CHRISTIAN PERSPECTIVES ON RESTORATIVE JUSTICE

Faith-Based Restorative Justice: Christian Principles and Practices

Dr. Maxwell Shimba

Printed in the United States of America

SHIMBA
PUBLISHING

TABLE OF CONTENTS

INTRODUCTION

Introduction: Understanding Restorative Justice from a Christian Perspective

Restorative justice represents a paradigm shift in the way we think about crime and punishment. Unlike the traditional retributive justice system, which focuses on punishment and deterrence, restorative justice emphasizes healing, reconciliation, and the restoration of relationships between victims, offenders, and the community. It seeks to address the harm caused by criminal behavior in a manner that promotes forgiveness, accountability, and transformation.

In a world where the criminal justice system often seems impersonal and punitive, restorative justice offers a more humane and compassionate alternative. It recognizes that crime causes real harm to people and communities and that the most effective response is one that seeks to repair that harm rather than simply punish the offender. This approach resonates deeply with the core principles of Christianity, which emphasize forgiveness, reconciliation, and the inherent worth of every individual.

Definition of Restorative Justice

Restorative justice can be broadly defined as a process that seeks to involve all stakeholders affected by an offense in collectively identifying and addressing the harm, needs, and obligations created by the offense. This process is designed to heal and put right the wrongs in a way that addresses the needs of the victim, holds the offender accountable, and engages the community in the process of restoration.

Key elements of restorative justice include:

1. Inclusion of All Parties: Restorative justice involves victims, offenders, and the community in a collaborative process. This inclusion ensures that all voices are heard and that the needs and perspectives of all parties are considered.

2. Focus on Harm and Needs: The primary focus is on addressing the harm caused by the offense and meeting the needs of those affected. This contrasts with the traditional justice system, which often focuses solely on determining guilt and imposing punishment.

3. Accountability and Responsibility: Offenders are encouraged to take responsibility for their actions and to understand the impact of their behavior on others. This accountability is seen as a crucial step in the process of rehabilitation and reconciliation.

4. Reparation and Healing: Restorative justice seeks to repair the harm caused by the offense through various means, including apologies, restitution, and community service. The goal is to promote healing for victims, offenders, and the broader community.

The Importance of Restorative Justice in Christian Thought

Restorative justice aligns closely with Christian teachings on justice, forgiveness, and reconciliation. The Bible is replete with examples of restorative principles. In the Old Testament, the concept of justice often includes the idea of restitution and restoration (Exodus 22:1-14; Leviticus 6:1-7). The New Testament further emphasizes the importance of forgiveness and reconciliation, with Jesus' teachings in the Sermon on the Mount (Matthew 5-7) and the apostle Paul's letters underscoring the need for believers to seek peace and restore relationships (Romans 12:17-21; 2 Corinthians 5:18-20).

Christians are called to reflect the character of God, who is described as just, merciful, and loving. This divine justice is not merely about retribution but about restoring right relationships and healing brokenness. The parable of the prodigal son (Luke 15:11-32) is a powerful illustration of God's restorative justice, where the focus is on the restoration of a broken relationship rather than punishment for wrongdoing.

The Journey Ahead

In the chapters that follow, we will explore the concept of restorative justice from various angles within the Christian tradition. We will examine its biblical foundations, theological underpinnings, historical applications, and contemporary practices. By doing so, we hope to provide a comprehensive understanding of how restorative justice not only aligns with Christian values but also offers a transformative approach to addressing harm and fostering reconciliation in our communities.

As we embark on this journey, we invite you to consider how restorative justice can be a reflection of God's justice in the world. May this exploration inspire and challenge you to embrace restorative principles in your own life and community, promoting healing, reconciliation, and the restoration of relationships in a manner that honors God and embodies the love of Christ.

Importance of the Topic within Christian Ethics and Theology

Restorative justice is not merely a contemporary social innovation; it is deeply embedded in the moral and theological fabric of Christianity. Understanding its significance within Christian ethics and theology is essential for several reasons.

Reflecting God's Character

At the heart of Christian belief is the nature of God, who is described as just, merciful, and loving. God's justice is restorative rather than merely punitive. Throughout the Bible, God is portrayed as a being who seeks to restore broken relationships and heal the wounds caused by sin. This is evident in the narratives of redemption and reconciliation that run through both the Old and New Testaments. For instance, the story of Israel's redemption from exile and the life and teachings of Jesus Christ both illustrate a divine preference for restoring relationships and communities over exacting retribution. Thus, restorative justice reflects the very character of God, making it a vital aspect of Christian ethics.

Biblical Foundations

The Bible provides numerous examples and principles that align with restorative justice. In the Old Testament, laws given to Israel often included provisions for restitution and reconciliation. For example, the Mosaic Law prescribed that if someone stole an ox or a sheep, they were to repay it multiple times over, demonstrating a concern for restitution and restoration (Exodus 22:1). Moreover, the Year of Jubilee (Leviticus 25) was a time of economic and social restoration, where debts were forgiven, and slaves were freed, embodying a holistic vision of justice that goes beyond punishment to include mercy and restoration.

In the New Testament, Jesus' ministry was marked by a commitment to restoring broken lives and relationships. His teachings on forgiveness, such as the parable of the unmerciful servant (Matthew 18:21-35), and His own actions, like His interactions with Zacchaeus (Luke 19:1-10), emphasize the importance of reconciliation and restoration. The Apostle Paul also highlights the ministry of reconciliation, urging believers to be ambassadors of God's restorative justice (2 Corinthians 5:18-20).

Ethical Mandate for Christians

Christian ethics, grounded in the teachings of Jesus, calls believers to pursue justice in a way that promotes peace and reconciliation. This ethical mandate is particularly evident in the Sermon on the Mount, where Jesus teaches about the blessedness of peacemakers (Matthew 5:9) and the importance of reconciling with others before offering gifts at the altar (Matthew 5:23-24). These teachings challenge Christians to go beyond seeking retribution and instead actively work towards healing and restoring relationships.

Restorative justice provides a practical framework for living out these ethical imperatives. By prioritizing the needs of victims, encouraging offenders to take responsibility, and involving the community in the process of healing, restorative justice embodies the Christian call to love one's neighbor and seek the common good. It transforms abstract ethical principles into tangible actions that foster peace and reconciliation in society.

Addressing Modern Challenges

In a world marked by increasing polarization, violence, and systemic injustices, restorative justice offers a hopeful alternative that aligns with Christian values. Traditional punitive approaches to justice often fail to address the underlying causes of crime and do little to heal the wounds inflicted on victims and communities. Restorative justice, on the other hand, seeks to address these root causes, promote accountability, and facilitate genuine healing.

For the Christian community, embracing restorative justice means engaging with contemporary social issues in a way that reflects Christ's teachings. It involves advocating for justice systems that prioritize restoration over retribution and actively participating in efforts to heal and reconcile broken relationships. This engagement not only addresses the immediate needs of those affected by crime but also witnesses to the transformative power of God's love and justice in the world.

A Call to Action

Understanding the importance of restorative justice within Christian ethics and theology is not an end in itself but a call to action. Christians are invited to embody the principles of restorative justice in their personal lives, their communities, and their advocacy for broader societal change. By doing so, they bear witness to the redemptive work of Christ and contribute to building a more just and compassionate world.

As we delve deeper into the theological and practical dimensions of restorative justice in the following chapters, may we be inspired to live out this call with courage and conviction?Restorative justice is not just a theoretical concept but a tangible expression of God's kingdom on earth, where peace, healing, and reconciliation are pursued with unwavering commitment.

DR. MAXWELL SHIMBA

CHAPTER 01

BIBLICAL FOUNDATIONS OF JUSTICE

Overview of Justice in the Old Testament

The concept of justice in the Old Testament is multifaceted, encompassing a range of practices and principles designed to maintain social order, protect the vulnerable, and reflect the character of God. Understanding Old Testament justice requires an examination of its legal codes, narratives, and prophetic literature, which together reveal a complex interplay between retributive and restorative elements. This chapter will explore these dimensions and consider the question of whether Old Testament justice was predominantly retributive.

Justice as Covenant Faithfulness

At the heart of Old Testament justice is the covenant relationship between God and Israel. This covenant, established at Sinai, defined Israel's identity and ethical responsibilities. Justice, in this context, was not merely a legal matter but a covenantal obligation. The Hebrew word for justice, mishpat, is closely linked with tzedakah, often translated as righteousness. Together, they reflect a vision of justice that is deeply relational and rooted in fidelity to God's commands.

Legal Codes: Retributive and Restorative Elements

The Old Testament legal codes, particularly those found in Exodus, Leviticus, and Deuteronomy, contain both retributive and restorative elements. Retributive justice, which emphasizes punishment proportionate to the offense, is evident in laws such as "an eye for an eye" (Exodus 21:24). This principle of lex talionis was intended to limit retribution and prevent excessive punishment. However, it was also complemented by laws designed to restore relationships and provide restitution.

For example, the law concerning theft required the thief to make restitution to the victim, often paying back more than what was stolen (Exodus 22:1-4). This not only punished the offender but also sought to restore what was lost and reconcile the parties involved. Similarly, the laws concerning injuries and damages often included provisions for compensation and reconciliation (Leviticus 24:19-20; Exodus 21:18-36).

Justice for the Vulnerable

A significant aspect of Old Testament justice is its concern for the vulnerable—widows, orphans, foreigners, and the poor. Numerous laws and prophetic exhortations emphasize the protection and provision for these groups. For instance, the gleaning laws required landowners to leave the edges of their fields unharvested so that the poor could gather food (Leviticus 19:9-10; Deuteronomy 24:19-21). This not only provided for the needy but also promoted a sense of community responsibility and care.

The Sabbath and Jubilee years further illustrate this restorative dimension. Every seventh year, debts were to be forgiven, and Hebrew slaves were to be released (Deuteronomy 15:1-18). Every fiftieth year, the Year of Jubilee, involved the return of land to its original owners, ensuring that economic disparities did not become permanent and that families could regain their ancestral inheritance (Leviticus 25:8-55). These practices aimed at restoring social and economic balance and preventing the perpetuation of poverty and injustice.

Prophetic Calls for Justice

The prophets played a crucial role in articulating and enforcing the vision of justice in the Old Testament. They often critiqued Israel's leaders and people for failing to uphold justice and righteousness. The prophets Amos, Micah, Isaiah, and Jeremiah, among others, condemned the exploitation of the poor, corruption, and the perversion of justice.

Amos famously declared, "But let justice roll on like a river, righteousness like a never-failing stream!" (Amos 5:24), calling for a society where justice and righteousness are pervasive. Micah summarized the ethical demands of the covenant with the words, "He has shown you, O mortal, what is good. And what does the Lord require of you? To act justly and to love mercy and to walk humbly with your God" (Micah 6:8). These prophetic voices emphasize that true justice is holistic, combining legal rectitude with mercy, humility, and social equity.

Retributive vs. Restorative Justice

While the Old Testament includes clear examples of retributive justice, its overarching vision is profoundly restorative. Retributive justice was intended to maintain order and deter wrongdoing, but it was always embedded within a larger framework that sought to restore relationships, repair harm, and promote community well-being. The sacrificial system itself, with its provisions for atonement and reconciliation, reflects a restorative approach. Sin offerings and guilt offerings were not merely punitive but were intended to restore the sinner to a right relationship with God and the community (Leviticus 4-5).

Moreover, the emphasis on forgiveness, restitution, and communal responsibility points to a justice system that values restoration as much as retribution. The frequent calls to care for the vulnerable and the institutionalized practices of Sabbath and Jubilee highlight a commitment to social and economic justice that transcends mere retribution.

Conclusion

The justice system of the Old Testament is a rich tapestry that weaves together retributive and restorative elements, reflecting the complex nature of God's justice. While retribution plays a role in maintaining social order and deterring crime, the broader vision of Old Testament justice is one of restoration, reconciliation, and the promotion of righteousness and community well-being.

As we consider the implications of this for contemporary Christian thought and practice, it becomes clear that a biblical approach to justice cannot be confined to punitive measures alone. Instead, it must encompass a holistic vision that seeks to heal and restore, reflecting the character of a just and merciful God. This foundational understanding will guide our exploration of restorative justice within the Christian tradition in the chapters that follow.

Jesus' Teachings on Justice and Reconciliation

Jesus' teachings on justice and reconciliation represent a profound and transformative understanding of these concepts, rooted deeply in the Old Testament but expanded and enriched through His ministry. This chapter explores how Jesus' teachings not only reaffirm but also fulfill and transcend Old Testament laws, presenting a holistic vision of justice and reconciliation that continues to inspire and challenge Christians today. We will also address the critical question: Did Jesus change the Old Testament laws?

Justice in Jesus' Ministry

From the outset of His ministry, Jesus made it clear that His mission was to bring about a new understanding of God's kingdom, which included a radical approach to justice and reconciliation. In Luke 4:18-19, Jesus reads from the scroll of Isaiah, proclaiming:

> "The Spirit of the Lord is on me,

> because he has anointed me

> to proclaim good news to the poor.

> He has sent me to proclaim freedom for the prisoners

> and recovery of sight for the blind,

> to set the oppressed free,

> to proclaim the year of the Lord's favor."

This proclamation sets the tone for Jesus' ministry, emphasizing justice for the marginalized and oppressed, aligning closely with Old Testament themes of social justice and divine mercy.

The Sermon on the Mount

One of the most comprehensive collections of Jesus' teachings on justice and reconciliation is found in the Sermon on the Mount (Matthew 5-7). Here, Jesus addresses a wide array of ethical and moral issues, providing a deepened and intensified interpretation of Old Testament laws.

The Beatitudes

The Beatitudes (Matthew 5:3-12) highlight the values of the kingdom of heaven, turning conventional notions of justice and power on their head. They bless the poor in spirit, those who mourn, the meek, those who hunger and thirst for righteousness, the merciful, the pure in heart, the peacemakers, and those persecuted for righteousness. These blessings underscore a justice that is compassionate, inclusive, and deeply concerned with the well-being of the vulnerable.

Fulfillment of the Law

Jesus explicitly states His relationship to the Old Testament laws in Matthew 5:17-20:

> "Do not think that I have come to abolish the Law or the Prophets; I have not come to abolish them but to fulfill them. For truly I tell you, until heaven and earth disappear, not the smallest letter, not the least stroke of a pen, will by any means disappear from the Law until everything is accomplished. Therefore anyone who sets aside one of the least of these commands and teaches others accordingly will be called least in the kingdom of heaven, but whoever practices and teaches these commands will be called great in the kingdom of heaven. For I tell you that unless your righteousness surpasses that of the Pharisees and the teachers of the law, you will certainly not enter the kingdom of heaven."

This passage is crucial in understanding that Jesus did not come to abolish the law but to fulfill it, indicating that His teachings bring the full meaning and purpose of the law to light. He emphasizes a righteousness that goes beyond mere legalistic adherence to the law, pointing towards a transformative internalization of God's will.

Deepening the Law

Jesus then proceeds to deepen the understanding of several Old Testament laws. For example:

- Anger and Reconciliation (Matthew 5:21-26): Jesus extends the commandment against murder to include anger and insults, emphasizing the importance of reconciliation. He teaches that being reconciled with others is so vital that it should take precedence over religious rituals.

- Adultery and Lust (Matthew 5:27-30): He expands the prohibition of adultery to include lustful thoughts, underscoring the importance of inner purity and integrity.

- Love for Enemies (Matthew 5:43-48): Jesus calls for love towards enemies and prayer for persecutors, radically transforming the understanding of love and justice from retribution to mercy and grace.

Parables on Justice and Reconciliation

Jesus' parables often illustrate principles of justice and reconciliation in vivid, relatable ways. Some notable examples include:

The Parable of the Good Samaritan

In the Parable of the Good Samaritan (Luke 10:25-37), Jesus redefines the concept of neighbor and challenges the social and ethnic boundaries of His time. The Samaritan, considered an outsider and enemy, is the one who shows mercy and acts justly, emphasizing that true justice transcends societal prejudices and extends compassion to all in need.

The Parable of the Prodigal Son

The Parable of the Prodigal Son (Luke 15:11-32) is a profound narrative of reconciliation. The father's unconditional forgiveness and joyful restoration of his wayward son illustrate divine grace and the priority of restoring broken relationships. This parable highlights that justice in God's kingdom involves forgiveness and the restoration of relationships, rather than punishment.

The Parable of the Unmerciful Servant

In the Parable of the Unmerciful Servant (Matthew 18:21-35), Jesus teaches about the necessity of forgiveness. The king forgives an enormous debt, but the forgiven servant refuses to forgive a small debt owed to him. This parable underscores the importance of extending the mercy we receive from God to others, making forgiveness a critical aspect of justice and reconciliation.

Jesus and the Old Testament Laws

The question of whether Jesus changed the Old Testament laws is complex. Jesus affirmed the validity and enduring relevance of the Old Testament laws but also brought a deeper, more profound understanding of them. He emphasized the spirit of the law over the letter, focusing on the intentions and attitudes of the heart rather than mere external compliance.

For example, in His approach to the Sabbath, Jesus emphasized the principle of mercy over strict Sabbath observance. He declared, "The Sabbath was made for man, not man for the Sabbath. So the Son of Man is Lord even of the Sabbath" (Mark 2:27-28). Here, Jesus did not abolish the Sabbath law but reoriented its observance towards human well-being and mercy.

Similarly, His teaching on divorce in Matthew 19:3-9 reaffirms the sanctity of marriage while acknowledging the hardness of human hearts that necessitated certain allowances in the Mosaic Law. Jesus' approach consistently aimed to restore the original intent and righteousness behind the laws.

Conclusion

Jesus' teachings on justice and reconciliation are deeply rooted in the Old Testament but also bring a transformative depth and clarity that fulfill and transcend the old laws. His ministry emphasizes a justice that is not merely retributive but restorative, aiming to heal and reconcile rather than simply punish. Through His teachings and parables, Jesus calls His followers to a higher standard of righteousness, characterized by mercy, forgiveness, and love.

By fulfilling the Old Testament laws and revealing their fullest meaning, Jesus provides a comprehensive and compelling vision of justice that challenges Christians to embody these principles in their lives and communities. As we continue to explore the implications of restorative justice within the Christian tradition, Jesus' teachings serve as a foundational guide and inspiration for seeking justice that truly reflects God's kingdom.

Pauline Theology and Justice

Paul the Apostle's writings have significantly shaped Christian theology and ethics, including concepts of justice. His letters reflect a complex and nuanced understanding of justice that integrates elements of retributive and restorative justice, deeply influenced by his Jewish heritage and transformative encounter with Christ. This chapter explores Paul's theology of justice, his application of these principles in the cases of Philemon and Onesimus, the Corinthian church, and the broader theological framework in the book of Romans.

Pauline Theology and Justice

Pauline theology reflects a profound understanding of justice that encompasses God's righteousness (dikaiosynē) and human ethical conduct. For Paul, justice is both a divine attribute and a moral imperative for believers. This dual aspect is rooted in the Old Testament's portrayal of God as just and righteous, but it is transformed through the lens of Christ's redemptive work.

Paul's theology of justice can be summarized in several key themes:

1. Justification by Faith: Central to Paul's teaching is the concept of justification by faith, where believers are declared righteous by God's grace through faith in Christ (Romans 3:21-26). This divine act of justice emphasizes God's righteousness and mercy, reconciling sinners to Himself.

2. New Creation: In Christ, believers become a new creation (2 Corinthians 5:17), which entails a transformation of ethical behavior. Justice, therefore, is not only a legal declaration but a transformative process that renews individuals and communities.

3. Reconciliation: Paul emphasizes reconciliation, both between humanity and God and among individuals. This theme is evident in his calls for unity, forgiveness, and mutual support within the Christian community.

4. Ethical Living: Paul's letters frequently address ethical conduct, urging believers to live justly, love mercy, and walk humbly with God (cf. Micah 6:8, Romans 12:1-2). This practical outworking of justice reflects the moral standards of the new covenant community.

Case of Philemon and Onesimus

The letter to Philemon provides a poignant case study of Paul's approach to justice and reconciliation. Onesimus, a runaway slave who had wronged his master Philemon, encounters Paul and becomes a Christian. Paul writes to

Philemon, urging him to receive Onesimus not as a slave but as a beloved brother in Christ.

Key Points in Philemon

- Appeal to Love and Fellowship: Paul appeals to Philemon on the basis of love and fellowship rather than asserting apostolic authority. He writes, "Therefore, although in Christ I could be bold and order you to do what you ought to do, yet I prefer to appeal to you on the basis of love" (Philemon 8-9).

- Transformation of Status: Paul highlights the transformative power of the gospel in Onesimus's life, urging Philemon to see him as a brother. "Perhaps the reason he was separated from you for a little while was that you might have him back forever—no longer as a slave, but better than a slave, as a dear brother" (Philemon 15-16).

- Restorative Justice: Paul's request embodies restorative justice, seeking to restore the broken relationship between Philemon and Onesimus and reintegrate Onesimus into the Christian community with a new identity and status.

Justice in the Corinthian Church

Paul's letters to the Corinthians address various issues of justice within the church community, including divisions, immorality, and lawsuits among believers.

Addressing Divisions and Immorality

- Unity and Love: Paul emphasizes unity and mutual edification within the church, countering factions and divisions. He writes, "I appeal to you, brothers and sisters, in the name of our Lord Jesus Christ, that all of you agree with one another in what you say and that there be no divisions among you, but that you be perfectly united in mind and thought" (1 Corinthians 1:10).

- Sexual Immorality: Addressing sexual immorality, Paul insists on ethical conduct that reflects the holiness of God. He warns against behaviors that harm the community and dishonor God, urging the Corinthians to flee from immorality and honor God with their bodies (1 Corinthians 6:18-20).

Lawsuits Among Believers

- Internal Resolution: Paul criticizes the Corinthians for taking their disputes before secular courts instead of resolving them within the church. He asks, "If any of you has a dispute with another, do you dare to take it before the ungodly for judgment instead of before the Lord's people?" (1 Corinthians 6:1). Paul advocates for a restorative approach, encouraging believers to resolve conflicts in a manner that reflects their new identity in Christ and the values of the Christian community.

Paul's Method of Justice in Romans

The book of Romans provides a comprehensive theological framework for understanding Paul's concept of justice. It addresses the righteousness of God, human sinfulness, and the means of justification and sanctification.

God's Righteousness and Human Sinfulness

- Universal Sinfulness: Paul begins by establishing the universal need for God's justice due to human sinfulness. "For all have sinned and fall short of the glory of God" (Romans 3:23). This underscores the need for divine intervention to restore justice.

- Justification by Faith: Central to Romans is the doctrine of justification by faith. Paul explains that through faith in Jesus Christ, believers are justified and made righteous before God. "But now apart from the law the righteousness of God has been made known... This righteousness is given through faith in Jesus Christ to all who believe" (Romans 3:21-22).

Justice in the New Life

- Living Sacrifices: Paul calls believers to live justly as a response to God's mercy. "Therefore, I urge you, brothers and sisters, in view of God's mercy, to offer your bodies as a living sacrifice, holy and pleasing to God—this is your true and proper worship" (Romans 12:1). This exhortation to ethical living is a practical outworking of God's justice in the believer's life.

- Love and Forgiveness: Paul emphasizes love as the fulfillment of the law and the guiding principle of Christian ethics. "Let no debt remain outstanding, except the continuing debt to love one another, for whoever loves others has fulfilled the law" (Romans 13:8).

Exhaustive Concordance References

Using a Strong's Exhaustive Concordance, we can delve deeper into key Greek terms used by Paul to articulate his concept of justice:

- Dikaiosynē (G1343): Often translated as "righteousness," it encompasses justice, virtue, and moral correctness. Found frequently in Romans (e.g., Romans 1:17, 3:21-22).

- Katallagē (G2643): Meaning "reconciliation," highlighting the restorative aspect of Paul's theology (e.g., Romans 5:11, 2 Corinthians 5:18-19).

- Charis (G5485): "Grace," emphasizing God's unmerited favor and foundational to justification by faith (e.g., Romans 3:24, 5:2).

Conclusion

Paul's theology of justice is deeply rooted in the righteousness of God, expressed through the life, death, and resurrection of Jesus Christ. It integrates elements of retributive and restorative justice, emphasizing both the legal declaration of righteousness and the ethical transformation of believers. Through his letters, Paul provides a comprehensive and practical framework for understanding and living out justice in the Christian community. His teachings on justification, reconciliation, and ethical living continue to inspire and challenge Christians to pursue a justice that reflects the character of God and the values of His kingdom.

Justice in the Corinthian Church

Paul's letters to the Corinthians, particularly 1 Corinthians and 2 Corinthians, provide a rich and detailed insight into the challenges faced by the early Christian community in Corinth. These letters address various issues related to justice within the church, including divisions, immorality, and lawsuits among believers. Paul's guidance on these matters not only aimed to resolve immediate conflicts but also to establish a framework for justice that reflected the principles of the Christian faith.

The Context of the Corinthian Church

Corinth was a major city in ancient Greece, known for its wealth, commerce, and diverse population. It was also notorious for its moral decadence and religious pluralism. The Christian community in Corinth reflected this diversity and faced significant challenges in maintaining unity and moral integrity amidst the surrounding culture.

Paul's correspondence with the Corinthians reveals a community struggling with internal divisions, ethical dilemmas, and a lack of understanding regarding the application of Christian principles to daily life. His letters serve as both corrective and instructional, aiming to guide the Corinthians towards a more just and unified expression of their faith.

Addressing Divisions

One of the primary issues Paul addresses is the existence of factions within the church. These divisions were based on allegiance to different leaders, which undermined the unity and witness of the Christian community.

Unity in Christ

Paul begins by emphasizing the centrality of Christ and the futility of dividing over human leaders. In 1 Corinthians 1:10-13, he writes:

> "I appeal to you, brothers and sisters, in the name of our Lord Jesus Christ, that all of you agree with one another in what you say and that there be no divisions among you, but that you be perfectly united in mind and thought. My brothers and sisters, some from Chloe's household have informed me that there are quarrels among you. What I mean

is this: One of you says, 'I follow Paul'; another, 'I follow Apollos'; another, 'I follow Cephas'; still another, 'I follow Christ.' Is Christ divided? Was Paul crucified for you? Were you baptized in the name of Paul?"

Paul's rhetorical questions highlight the absurdity of dividing Christ's body based on human leadership. He calls the Corinthians to recognize their unity in Christ, who alone is the foundation of their faith and community.

The Role of Leaders

Paul also addresses the proper role of church leaders, emphasizing that they are merely servants of God, not figures to be idolized. In 1 Corinthians 3:5-7, he writes:

> "What, after all, is Apollos? And what is Paul? Only servants, through whom you came to believe—as the Lord has assigned to each his task. I planted the seed, Apollos watered it, but God has been making it grow. So neither the one who plants nor the one who waters is anything, but only God, who makes things grow."

By redirecting the focus to God, Paul seeks to dismantle the causes of division and promote a spirit of unity and cooperation within the church.

Addressing Immorality

The moral standards of the Corinthian church were significantly influenced by the surrounding culture, which led to various ethical issues, including sexual immorality.

Condemnation of Immorality

In 1 Corinthians 5, Paul confronts a specific case of sexual immorality within the church, where a man is living with his father's wife. He expresses shock and dismay at the church's tolerance of such behavior:

> "It is actually reported that there is sexual immorality among you, and of a kind that even pagans do not tolerate: A man is sleeping with his father's wife. And you are proud! Shouldn't you rather have gone into mourning and have put out of your fellowship the man who has been doing this?" (1 Corinthians 5:1-2).

Paul's response is firm and uncompromising. He instructs the church to expel the immoral brother to protect the community's moral integrity and witness (1 Corinthians 5:13). This disciplinary action is intended to lead to the offender's repentance and eventual restoration.

Call to Holiness

Paul further emphasizes the importance of holiness and moral purity in the Christian life. In 1 Corinthians 6:18-20, he writes:

> "Flee from sexual immorality. All other sins a person commits are outside the body, but whoever sins sexually, sins against their own body. Do you not know that your bodies are temples of the Holy Spirit, who is in you, whom you have received from God? You are not your own; you were bought at a price. Therefore honor God with your bodies."

By framing the body as a temple of the Holy Spirit, Paul elevates the standard of personal conduct and calls believers to live in a manner that honors God.

Lawsuits Among Believers

Another issue Paul addresses is the practice of believers taking their disputes to secular courts rather than resolving them within the church.

Internal Resolution of Disputes

In 1 Corinthians 6:1-8, Paul criticizes the Corinthians for airing their grievances before unbelievers:

> "If any of you has a dispute with another, do you dare to take it before the ungodly for judgment instead of before the Lord's people? Or do you not know that the Lord's people will judge the world? And if you are to judge the world, are you not competent to judge trivial cases? Do you not know that we will judge angels? How much more the things of this life! Therefore, if you have disputes about such

matters, do you ask for a ruling from those whose way of life is scorned in the church? I say this to shame you. Is it possible that there is nobody among you wise enough to judge a dispute between believers? But instead, one brother takes another to court—and this in front of unbelievers!"

Paul's concern is twofold: the witness of the church to the outside world and the capability of the church to handle internal matters. He argues that Christians, who are destined to judge the world and even angels, should be competent to resolve their own disputes.

Emphasis on Forgiveness and Reconciliation

Paul also highlights the importance of forgiveness and reconciliation, urging believers to endure wrongs rather than seeking retribution:

> "The very fact that you have lawsuits among you means you have been completely defeated already. Why not rather be wronged? Why not rather be cheated? Instead, you yourselves cheat and do wrong, and you do this to your brothers and sisters." (1 Corinthians 6:7-8).

Paul's radical call to absorb wrongs and prioritize reconciliation reflects the transformative ethic of the gospel, where justice is not merely about retribution but about restoring relationships and community harmony.

Theological Foundations

Paul's instructions to the Corinthians are rooted in a theological framework that emphasizes the transformative power of the gospel. This framework includes the concepts of justification, sanctification, and the new creation.

Justification and Sanctification

Paul's theology of justification by faith (Romans 3:21-26) undergirds his approach to justice in the church. Believers are declared righteous through faith in Christ, which transforms their status and identity. This justification is not merely a legal declaration but initiates a process of sanctification—being made holy—that affects all aspects of life, including ethical conduct and community relationships.

New Creation

The concept of the new creation is central to Paul's ethical teachings. In 2 Corinthians 5:17, he writes:

> "Therefore, if anyone is in Christ, the new creation has come: The old has gone, the new is here!"

This new identity in Christ calls believers to live according to the values of the new creation, characterized by love, justice, and reconciliation. The community of believers is to reflect the kingdom of God, where justice is restorative and relationships are marked by forgiveness and unity.

Conclusion

Paul's letters to the Corinthians provide a comprehensive and practical guide to justice within the Christian community. He addresses issues of divisions, immorality, and disputes with a focus on unity, holiness, and reconciliation. His instructions are grounded in a robust theological framework that emphasizes the transformative power of the gospel and the new identity of believers in Christ.

By calling the Corinthians to a higher standard of justice that reflects the principles of the kingdom of God, Paul offers timeless guidance for the church today. His teachings challenge believers to embody a justice that is not only fair and righteous but also deeply compassionate and restorative, aligning with the character and mission of Christ.

Paul's Method of Justice in Romans

The book of Romans is a cornerstone of Christian theology, providing a profound and comprehensive explanation of Paul's understanding of justice. In Romans, Paul addresses key theological themes such as the righteousness of God, human sinfulness, justification by faith, and sanctification. These concepts are intricately woven together to present a coherent and transformative vision of justice that transcends mere legalism and embraces the holistic redemption offered through Jesus Christ.

The Righteousness of God

Paul begins his letter to the Romans by establishing the righteousness of God as the foundation of his theological framework. This righteousness (dikaiosynē theou) is a key theme throughout the letter, highlighting God's just character and His actions in human history.

Revelation of God's Righteousness

In Romans 1:16-17, Paul writes:

> "For I am not ashamed of the gospel, because it is the power of God that brings salvation to everyone who believes: first to the Jew, then to the Gentile. For in the gospel the righteousness of God is revealed—a righteousness that is by faith from first to last, just as it is written: 'The righteous will live by faith.'"

Here, Paul declares that the gospel reveals the righteousness of God, which is accessible through faith. This righteousness is not merely a divine attribute but an active force that brings about salvation and transformation in the lives of believers.

The Universality of Sin

Paul then contrasts God's righteousness with the universal sinfulness of humanity. In Romans 3:23, he states:

> "For all have sinned and fall short of the glory of God."

This stark assessment underscores the need for divine intervention. Human beings, regardless of their background, are incapable of achieving righteousness on their own due to their inherent sinfulness. This sets the stage for Paul's discussion on justification and the transformative justice of God.

Justification by Faith

Central to Paul's theology in Romans is the doctrine of justification by faith. Justification (dikaiosis) refers to being declared righteous before God, and it is a key component of Paul's understanding of justice.

Justification as a Gift of Grace

In Romans 3:24-26, Paul explains:

> "And all are justified freely by his grace through the redemption that came by Christ Jesus. God presented Christ as a sacrifice of atonement, through the shedding of his blood—to be received by faith. He did this to demonstrate his righteousness because in his forbearance he had left the sins committed beforehand unpunished—he did it to demonstrate his righteousness at the present time, so as to be just and the one who justifies those who have faith in Jesus."

This passage highlights several critical points:

- Justification is a free gift of God's grace, not something earned by human effort.

- It is made possible through the sacrificial death of Jesus Christ, who bore the penalty for sin.

- This act of justification demonstrates God's righteousness and justice, as He remains just while justifying sinners.

Faith and the Example of Abraham

Paul further illustrates justification by faith using the example of Abraham. In Romans 4:3, he quotes Genesis 15:6:

> "Abraham believed God, and it was credited to him as righteousness."

Abraham's faith, not his works, was the basis for his righteousness. This principle of faith as the means of justification is extended to all believers, both Jews and Gentiles, emphasizing the inclusivity and universality of God's justice.

The Role of the Law

Paul's discussion of the law is crucial to understanding his concept of justice. He addresses the law's purpose, its limitations, and its fulfillment in Christ.

The Law and Human Sinfulness

In Romans 3:20, Paul states:

> "Therefore no one will be declared righteous in God's sight by the works of the law; rather, through the law we become conscious of our sin."

The law reveals human sinfulness but cannot provide the means for achieving righteousness. It serves as a mirror, reflecting humanity's moral failures and highlighting the need for a savior.

The Fulfillment of the Law in Christ

In Romans 10:4, Paul writes:

> "Christ is the culmination of the law so that there may be righteousness for everyone who believes."

Jesus fulfills the law's requirements and embodies its ultimate purpose. Through His life, death, and resurrection, Jesus establishes a new covenant in which righteousness is based on faith rather than adherence to the law.

Sanctification and Ethical Living

Paul's concept of justice extends beyond justification to include sanctification—the process of being made holy. Sanctification involves ethical transformation and the renewal of one's mind and behavior.

Living Sacrifices

In Romans 12:1-2, Paul urges believers:

> "Therefore, I urge you, brothers and sisters, in view of God's mercy, to offer your bodies as a living sacrifice, holy and pleasing to God—this is your true and proper worship. Do not conform to the pattern of this world, but be transformed by the renewing of your mind. Then you will be

able to test and approve what God's will is—his good, pleasing and perfect will."

Believers are called to present themselves as living sacrifices, dedicating their lives to God's service. This involves a radical transformation of one's values and conduct, aligning with God's will and reflecting His justice in everyday life.

Love as the Fulfillment of the Law

Paul emphasizes love as the fundamental ethical principle that fulfills the law. In Romans 13:8-10, he writes:

> "Let no debt remain outstanding, except the continuing debt to love one another, for whoever loves others has fulfilled the law. The commandments, 'You shall not commit adultery,' 'You shall not murder,' 'You shall not steal,' 'You shall not covet,' and whatever other command there may be, are summed up in this one command: 'Love your neighbor as yourself.' Love does no harm to a neighbor. Therefore love is the fulfillment of the law."

By prioritizing love, Paul reorients the law's demands towards relational ethics, where justice is expressed through genuine care and respect for others.

Exhaustive Strong's Concordance References

To delve deeper into Paul's method of justice in Romans, we can use Strong's Exhaustive Concordance to explore key Greek terms:

- Dikaiosynē (G1343): Righteousness, justice. Found in passages such as Romans 1:17, 3:21-22, and 10:4, highlighting God's righteous nature and the righteousness imparted to believers.

- Pistis (G4102): Faith. Central to the concept of justification by faith, found in Romans 1:17, 3:22, and 4:3.

- Nomos (G3551): Law. Refers to the Mosaic Law and its role in revealing sin and pointing to Christ, discussed extensively in Romans 2-8.

- Charis (G5485): Grace. Emphasized in Romans 3:24, 5:2, and 6:14 as the basis for justification and the transformative power in believers' lives.

Conclusion

Paul's method of justice in Romans presents a profound and holistic understanding of God's righteousness and human redemption. Through the themes of justification by faith, the role of the law, and the ethical transformation of believers, Paul articulates a vision of justice that is deeply rooted in God's character and redemptive plan. This justice is not merely about legal adherence but involves a transformative relationship with God, characterized by faith, grace, and love.

As we continue to explore the implications of Paul's theology for contemporary Christian thought and practice, the book of Romans serves as a foundational guide, challenging believers to embody a justice that reflects the heart of the gospel and the transformative power of Christ.

The Case of Philemon and Onesimus

The letter to Philemon is one of the shortest books in the New Testament, but it provides a powerful and nuanced example of Paul's approach to justice and reconciliation. This personal letter, written by Paul to a Christian named Philemon, addresses the situation of Onesimus, a runaway slave who has become a believer. Paul's appeal to Philemon to receive Onesimus not merely as a returning slave but as a beloved brother in Christ encapsulates key elements of Christian justice, mercy, and reconciliation. This chapter explores the context, content, and implications of this letter.

Historical and Social Context

Slavery in the Roman Empire

Slavery was a common and accepted institution in the Roman Empire, where slaves were considered property of their masters with few legal rights. The social and economic structure of the time depended heavily on slave labor. Within this context, a runaway slave like Onesimus would have faced severe punishment, and his return could have resulted in harsh consequences.

The Christian Community

The early Christian community was a diverse and inclusive group that often included both slaves and free individuals. The radical message of the gospel, which proclaimed equality and unity in Christ, challenged the existing social norms and hierarchies, including the institution of slavery. Paul's letter to Philemon must be understood against this backdrop of emerging Christian ethics and the transformative power of the gospel.

The Letter to Philemon

Introduction and Greetings

Paul begins his letter with a customary greeting that establishes his authority and sets a tone of warmth and affection:

> "Paul, a prisoner of Christ Jesus, and Timothy our brother, to Philemon our dear friend and fellow worker—also to Apphia our sister and Archippus our fellow soldier—and to the church that meets in your home: Grace and peace to you from God our Father and the Lord Jesus Christ." (Philemon 1-3)

By referring to himself as a "prisoner of Christ Jesus," Paul underscores his commitment to the gospel and his solidarity with those who suffer for their faith.

Thanksgiving and Prayer

Paul expresses his gratitude for Philemon's faith and love:

> "I always thank my God as I remember you in my prayers, because I hear about your love for all his holy people and your faith in the Lord Jesus. I pray that your partnership with us in the faith may be effective in deepening your understanding of every good thing we share for the sake of Christ. Your love has given me great joy and encouragement, because you, brother, have refreshed the hearts of the Lord's people." (Philemon 4-7)

This section not only affirms Philemon's character but also subtly prepares him for the request that follows by highlighting the importance of love and partnership in the faith.

Paul's Appeal for Onesimus

The heart of the letter is Paul's appeal on behalf of Onesimus:

> "Therefore, although in Christ I could be bold and order you to do what you ought to do, yet I prefer to appeal to you on the basis of love. It is as none other than Paul—an old man and now also a prisoner of Christ Jesus—that I appeal to you for my son Onesimus, who became my son while I was in chains. Formerly he was useless to you, but now

he has become useful both to you and to me." (Philemon 8-11)

Paul emphasizes love rather than authority, seeking to persuade Philemon through a heartfelt appeal rather than a command. He refers to Onesimus as "my son," indicating a deep personal bond and highlighting the transformative effect of the gospel on Onesimus's life.

Paul continues:

> "I am sending him—who is my very heart—back to you. I would have liked to keep him with me so that he could take your place in helping me while I am in chains for the gospel. But I did not want to do anything without your consent, so that any favor you do would not seem forced but would be voluntary." (Philemon 12-14)

Paul's language here underscores the depth of his affection for Onesimus and his desire for Philemon's voluntary cooperation in this matter.

Transformation and Reconciliation

Paul presents a theological reflection on the situation:

> "Perhaps the reason he was separated from you for a little while was that you might have him back forever—no longer as a slave, but better than a slave, as a dear brother. He

is very dear to me but even dearer to you, both as a fellow man and as a brother in the Lord." (Philemon 15-16)

This statement transforms the entire dynamic of the relationship. Paul suggests that the temporary separation had a divine purpose, leading to a permanent and profound transformation of Onesimus's status—from a slave to a beloved brother in Christ. This reflects the radical inclusivity of the Christian message, which transcends social and economic barriers.

Request for Reconciliation

Paul makes his final appeal:

> "So if you consider me a partner, welcome him as you would welcome me. If he has done you any wrong or owes you anything, charge it to me. I, Paul, am writing this with my own hand. I will pay it back—not to mention that you owe me your very self. I do wish, brother, that I may have some benefit from you in the Lord; refresh my heart in Christ. Confident of your obedience, I write to you, knowing that you will do even more than I ask." (Philemon 17-21)

Paul asks Philemon to receive Onesimus as he would receive Paul himself, signaling the depth of reconciliation and forgiveness he seeks. By offering to repay any debt Onesimus owes, Paul takes on the role of a mediator, embodying the sacrificial love and restorative justice central to the gospel.

Implications of Paul's Approach

Justice and Reconciliation

Paul's approach to the situation of Onesimus and Philemon provides a model of restorative justice. Rather than seeking retribution or merely addressing the legal aspects of Onesimus's status as a runaway slave, Paul emphasizes reconciliation and transformation. He envisions a new relationship based on mutual love and respect, reflecting the unity and equality found in Christ.

The Role of the Christian Community

Paul's letter also highlights the role of the Christian community in fostering justice and reconciliation. By addressing the letter to Philemon, Apphia, Archippus, and the church that meets in their home, Paul situates the individual case within the broader context of the Christian community. This collective responsibility underscores the importance of communal support and accountability in living out the principles of justice and reconciliation.

The Transformative Power of the Gospel

The case of Philemon and Onesimus illustrates the transformative power of the gospel to redefine relationships and social structures. In Christ, the distinctions between slave and free, master and servant, are transcended by a new identity as brothers and sisters. This radical reorientation challenges existing social norms and calls believers to live out the implications of their faith in concrete, relational terms.

Conclusion

The letter to Philemon offers a rich and nuanced example of Paul's approach to justice and reconciliation. Through his appeal on behalf of Onesimus, Paul models a form of justice that prioritizes reconciliation, transformation, and communal responsibility. This approach not only addresses the immediate situation but also provides a timeless framework for understanding and practicing justice within the Christian community. As we reflect on this case, we are reminded of the profound and transformative nature of the gospel, which calls us to embody justice, mercy, and love in our relationships and communities.

Paul's Justice to the Galatians

Paul's letter to the Galatians is a passionate defense of the gospel of grace and a sharp critique of those who sought to impose Jewish legal requirements on Gentile Christians. In addressing the Galatian crisis, Paul articulates a profound vision of justice rooted in faith, freedom, and the new creation in Christ. This chapter examines Paul's concept of justice as presented in Galatians, exploring themes such as justification by faith, the role of the law, Christian freedom, and the implications for community life and ethics.

Context of the Letter

The Galatian Crisis

The churches in Galatia were being influenced by Judaizers, who argued that Gentile converts must adhere to Jewish laws, particularly circumcision, to be fully accepted as Christians. This teaching threatened to undermine the gospel of grace that Paul had preached. Paul's letter to the Galatians addresses this controversy head-on, defending the sufficiency of faith in Christ for justification and condemning any return to legalism.

Paul's Apostolic Authority

Paul begins his letter by asserting his apostolic authority, emphasizing that his gospel came directly from Jesus Christ and not from human sources:

> "Paul, an apostle—sent not from men nor by a man, but by Jesus Christ and God the Father, who raised him from the dead—and all the brothers and sisters with me, to the churches in Galatia: Grace and peace to you from God our Father and the Lord Jesus Christ, who gave himself for our sins to rescue us from the present evil age, according to the will of our God and Father, to who be glory forever and ever. Amen." (Galatians 1:1-5)

This introduction sets the stage for Paul's urgent and authoritative response to the Galatian crisis.

Justification by Faith

The Heart of the Gospel

Central to Paul's message in Galatians is the doctrine of justification by faith. He argues that believers are justified—declared righteous—by faith in Jesus Christ, not by works of the law. This principle is articulated clearly in Galatians 2:15-16:

> "We who are Jews by birth and not sinful Gentiles know that a person is not justified by the works of the law but by faith in Jesus Christ. So we, too, have put our faith in Christ Jesus that we may be justified by faith in Christ and not by the works of the law because, by the works of the law, no one will be justified."

Paul's insistence on justification by faith alone is foundational to his concept of justice. It establishes that righteousness is a gift from God, received through faith, rather than something earned through human effort.

Abraham's Example

To reinforce his argument, Paul appeals to the example of Abraham, whose faith was credited to him as righteousness (Genesis 15:6). In Galatians 3:6-9, Paul writes:

> "So also Abraham 'believed God, and it was credited to him as righteousness.' Understand, then, that those who have faith are children of Abraham. Scripture foresaw that

God would justify the Gentiles by faith, and announced the gospel in advance to Abraham: 'All nations will be blessed through you.' So those who rely on faith are blessed along with Abraham, the man of faith."

By linking justification by faith to Abraham, Paul shows that this principle is deeply rooted in the scriptural narrative and applies to both Jews and Gentiles.

The Role of the Law

The Purpose of the Law

Paul acknowledges the significance of the law but redefines its role in the light of Christ. He argues that the law served a temporary purpose, acting as a guardian until Christ came. In Galatians 3:24-25, he explains:

> "So the law was our guardian until Christ came that we might be justified by faith. Now that this faith has come, we are no longer under a guardian."

The law revealed human sinfulness and pointed to the need for a savior. However, with the coming of Christ, believers are no longer bound by the law but are justified by faith in Him.

The Danger of Legalism

Paul warns the Galatians against reverting to legalism, which undermines the gospel of grace. He expresses his concern in Galatians 5:1-4:

> "It is for freedom that Christ has set us free. Stand firm, then, and do not let yourselves be burdened again by a yoke of slavery. Mark my words! I, Paul, tell you that if you let yourselves be circumcised, Christ will be of no value to you at all. Again I declare to every man who lets himself be circumcised that he is obligated to obey the whole law. You who are trying to be justified by the law have been alienated from Christ; you have fallen away from grace."

Paul's strong language underscores the gravity of the issue. Justification by the law is incompatible with the gospel of grace and leads to spiritual bondage.

Christian Freedom and Ethical Living

Freedom in Christ

For Paul, the freedom that comes from faith in Christ is central to the Christian life. This freedom is not a license to sin but a call to live by the Spirit. In Galatians 5:13-14, he writes:

> "You, my brothers and sisters, were called to be free. But do not use your freedom to indulge the flesh; rather, serve one another humbly in love. For the entire law is fulfilled in keeping this one command: 'Love your neighbor as yourself.'"

Paul redefines freedom as the ability to live in love and service to others, guided by the Holy Spirit.

The Fruit of the Spirit

Paul contrasts the works of the flesh with the fruit of the Spirit, providing a framework for ethical living. In Galatians 5:19-23, he states:

> "The acts of the flesh are obvious: sexual immorality, impurity, and debauchery; idolatry and witchcraft; hatred, discord, jealousy, fits of rage, selfish ambition, dissensions, factions, and envy; drunkenness, orgies, and the like. I warn you, as I did before, that those who live like this will not inherit the kingdom of God. But the fruit of the Spirit is love, joy, peace, forbearance, kindness, goodness, faithfulness, gentleness, and self-control. Against such things, there is no law."

By emphasizing the fruit of the Spirit, Paul shows that ethical living is the natural outflow of a life transformed by faith in Christ and led by the Spirit.

Implications for Community Life

Unity and Equality

Paul's vision of justice in Galatians includes a radical redefinition of social relationships within the Christian community. He emphasizes the equality and unity of all believers in Christ, regardless of ethnic, social, or gender distinctions. In Galatians 3:26-28, he declares:

> "So in Christ Jesus you are all children of God through faith, for all of you who were baptized into Christ have clothed yourselves with Christ. There is neither Jew nor Gentile, neither slave nor free, nor is there male and female, for you are all one in Christ Jesus."

This statement challenges the existing social hierarchies and promotes a vision of justice that is inclusive and egalitarian.

Bearing One Another's Burdens

Paul also highlights the importance of mutual support and accountability within the Christian community. In Galatians 6:1-2, he writes:

> "Brothers and sisters, if someone is caught in a sin, you who live by the Spirit should restore that person gently. But watch yourselves, or you also may be tempted. Carry each other's burdens, and in this way you will fulfill the law of Christ."

Restoring others gently and carrying each other's burdens exemplify the practical outworking of justice and love within the community.

Conclusion

Paul's letter to the Galatians presents a robust and dynamic vision of justice that is rooted in the gospel of grace and the transformative power of faith in Christ. By emphasizing justification by faith, the proper role of the law, Christian freedom, and ethical living, Paul articulates a justice that is both deeply personal and profoundly communal. His teachings challenge believers to reject legalism and embrace the freedom and responsibility of living by the Spirit, characterized by love, unity, and mutual support. As we reflect on Paul's message to the Galatians, we are invited to embody this justice in our own lives and communities, demonstrating the radical inclusivity and transformative power of the gospel.

Jesus' Sermon on the Mount - A Restorative Teaching

The Sermon on the Mount, found in Matthew 5-7, is one of the most profound and influential discourses given by Jesus. It encapsulates His teachings on ethics, justice, and the nature of the Kingdom of God. These teachings are deeply restorative, offering a vision of justice that goes beyond mere retribution and legalistic righteousness. Instead, Jesus presents a transformative approach that seeks to restore individuals and communities to their intended state of wholeness and righteousness.

The Beatitudes: Restoring the Marginalized

The Sermon begins with the Beatitudes (Matthew 5:3-12), a series of blessings that turn conventional values on their head and highlight God's special concern for the marginalized and oppressed.

Blessing the Poor in Spirit

> "Blessed are the poor in spirit, for theirs is the kingdom of heaven." (Matthew 5:3)

Jesus opens with a blessing on the "poor in spirit," those who recognize their spiritual poverty and dependence on God. This acknowledgment of need is the first step toward restoration, as it opens individuals to receive God's grace and healing.

Comforting Those Who Mourn

> "Blessed are those who mourn, for they will be comforted." (Matthew 5:4)

In a restorative context, this blessing assures those who are grieving that God sees their pain and will provide comfort. It reflects the restorative justice principle of acknowledging suffering and offering solace.

Elevating the Meek

> "Blessed are the meek, for they will inherit the earth." (Matthew 5:5)

The meek, often marginalized by society, are promised a place of honor in God's kingdom. This radical reordering of social values restores dignity and hope to those who are humble and gentle.

Satisfying the Hunger for Righteousness

> "Blessed are those who hunger and thirst for righteousness, for they will be filled." (Matthew 5:6)

Jesus affirms that those who earnestly seek justice and righteousness will be satisfied. This promise is deeply restorative, assuring that God's justice will prevail and that genuine efforts for righteousness will be rewarded.

Transforming Interpersonal Relationships

The Sermon on the Mount addresses various aspects of interpersonal relationships, emphasizing restoration and reconciliation over retaliation and retribution.

Anger and Reconciliation

> "You have heard that it was said to the people long ago, 'You shall not murder, and anyone who murders will be subject to judgment.' But I tell you that anyone who is angry with a brother or sister will be subject to judgment... Therefore, if you are offering your gift at the altar and there remember that your brother or sister has something against you, leave your gift there in front of the altar. First go and be reconciled to them; then come and offer your gift." (Matthew 5:21-24)

Jesus extends the commandment against murder to include anger and insults, highlighting the importance of restoring broken relationships. Reconciliation takes precedence over religious rituals, emphasizing the need for personal and communal harmony.

Adultery and Lust

> "You have heard that it was said, 'You shall not commit adultery.' But I tell you that anyone who looks at a woman lustfully has already committed adultery with her in his heart." (Matthew 5:27-28)

By addressing the internal attitudes that lead to sin, Jesus calls for a restoration of purity and respect in relationships. This deeper understanding of the law aims to prevent the harm caused by objectification and infidelity.

Divorce and Faithfulness

> "It has been said, 'Anyone who divorces his wife must give her a certificate of divorce.' But I tell you that anyone who divorces his wife, except for sexual immorality, makes her the victim of adultery, and anyone who marries a divorced woman commits adultery." (Matthew 5:31-32)

Jesus' teaching on divorce seeks to restore the sanctity and commitment of marriage. By challenging the permissive attitudes toward divorce, He emphasizes faithfulness and the well-being of all parties involved.

Oaths and Integrity

> "Again, you have heard that it was said to the people long ago, 'Do not break your oath, but fulfill to the Lord the

vows you have made.' But I tell you, do not swear an oath at all... All you need to say is simply 'Yes' or 'No'; anything beyond this comes from the evil one." (Matthew 5:33-37)

Jesus advocates for simplicity and integrity in speech, promoting a culture of honesty and trustworthiness. This teaching restores the value of one's word and fosters mutual respect in the community.

Embracing Radical Love and Forgiveness

Jesus' instructions on love and forgiveness are among the most radical and restorative aspects of the Sermon on the Mount.

Turning the Other Cheek

> "You have heard that it was said, 'Eye for eye, and tooth for tooth.' But I tell you, do not resist an evil person. If anyone slaps you on the right cheek, turn to them the other cheek also." (Matthew 5:38-39)

Jesus overturns the principle of retributive justice with a call to non-retaliation. This teaching aims to break the cycle of violence and restore peace, challenging individuals to respond to wrongdoing with grace and forbearance.

Loving Enemies

> "You have heard that it was said, 'Love your neighbor and hate your enemy.' But I tell you, love your

enemies and pray for those who persecute you, that you may be children of your Father in heaven." (Matthew 5:43-45)

Loving enemies and praying for persecutors represents a radical form of restorative justice. It seeks to heal relationships and transform adversaries through unconditional love and compassion.

Practicing Generosity and Compassion

> "Be careful not to practice your righteousness in front of others to be seen by them. If you do, you will have no reward from your Father in heaven... When you give to the needy, do not let your left hand know what your right hand is doing, so that your giving may be in secret. Then your Father, who sees what is done in secret, will reward you." (Matthew 6:1-4)

Jesus encourages acts of generosity and compassion to be done discreetly, fostering a genuine concern for the well-being of others. This practice restores dignity to the recipients of charity and emphasizes the intrinsic value of selfless love.

Restoring Relationship with God

Central to the Sermon on the Mount is the restoration of the individual's relationship with God.

Teaching on Prayer

> "This, then, is how you should pray: 'Our Father in heaven, hallowed be your name, your kingdom come, your

will be done, on earth as it is in heaven. Give us today our daily bread. And forgive us our debts, as we also have forgiven our debtors. And lead us not into temptation, but deliver us from the evil one.'" (Matthew 6:9-13)

The Lord's Prayer encapsulates a restorative relationship with God, emphasizing dependence, forgiveness, and deliverance. It aligns the believer's desires with God's will and fosters a sense of community through shared petitions.

Trusting in God's Provision

> "Therefore I tell you, do not worry about your life, what you will eat or drink; or about your body, what you will wear... But seek first his kingdom and his righteousness, and all these things will be given to you as well." (Matthew 6:25, 33)

Jesus teaches a radical trust in God's provision, encouraging believers to prioritize the pursuit of God's kingdom and righteousness. This trust restores peace and reduces anxiety, reinforcing the belief in God's care and sovereignty.

Establishing a Community of Justice and Peace

The Sermon on the Mount outlines principles for building a community that embodies restorative justice and peace.

Judging Others

> "Do not judge, or you too will be judged. For in the same way you judge others, you will be judged, and with the measure you use, it will be measured to you." (Matthew 7:1-2)

Jesus cautions against harsh judgment, promoting a community characterized by empathy and understanding. This teaching encourages self-reflection and humility, essential for restoring relationships.

The Golden Rule

> "So in everything, do to others what you would have them do to you, for this sums up the Law and the Prophets." (Matthew 7:12)

The Golden Rule encapsulates the essence of restorative justice, advocating for mutual respect and consideration. It fosters a culture of reciprocity and kindness, foundational for a just and peaceful community.

Building on a Solid Foundation

> "Therefore everyone who hears these words of mine and puts them into practice is like a wise man who built his house on the rock... But everyone who hears these words of mine and does not put them into practice is like a foolish man who built his house on sand." (Matthew 7:24, 26)

Jesus concludes the Sermon on the Mount by urging His listeners to act on His teachings, comparing their lives to houses built on solid or shaky foundations. Practicing these principles ensures a stable and resilient community rooted in justice and righteousness.

Conclusion

The Sermon on the Mount presents a transformative vision of justice that is deeply restorative. Jesus' teachings challenge individuals and communities to go beyond retributive justice and embrace principles that heal, reconcile, and restore. By addressing the needs of the marginalized, promoting integrity and love in relationships, and fostering a deep trust in God, Jesus outlines a blueprint for a community that reflects the values of the Kingdom of God. This restorative approach not only seeks to correct wrongs but to restore individuals and communities to their intended wholeness and righteousness, offering a powerful model for justice that transcends time and culture.

CHAPTER 02

THEOLOGICAL PERSPECTIVES

Catholic Views on Restorative Justice

Introduction

The Catholic Church has a rich and nuanced tradition of thought on justice, deeply rooted in its theological, philosophical, and social teachings. This chapter explores the Catholic perspective on restorative justice, examining its foundations in Scripture and Tradition, the teachings of key Church documents, and the practical implications for contemporary Catholic social ethics.

Foundations in Scripture and Tradition

Scriptural Basis

The Catholic view of justice is firmly rooted in the Scriptures, with a particular emphasis on the teachings of Jesus and the prophetic tradition of the Old Testament.

Old Testament Foundations

The Old Testament provides numerous examples of justice that emphasize both retributive and restorative elements. Key among these is the concept of shalom—a holistic peace that involves right relationships with God, others, and creation. The prophetic literature, especially in books like Isaiah, Amos, and Micah, calls for justice that rectifies social inequalities and restores community harmony.

Jesus' Teachings

Jesus' ministry, particularly His emphasis on forgiveness, mercy, and reconciliation, profoundly shapes the Catholic understanding of justice. The parable of the Prodigal Son (Luke 15:11-32), for instance, illustrates God's restorative approach to justice, highlighting forgiveness and the restoration of broken relationships.

Tradition and Church Fathers

Early Church Fathers, such as Augustine and Aquinas, developed a rich theological framework that integrates justice as a cardinal virtue essential for the moral life. Augustine viewed justice as a manifestation of love, while Aquinas' Summa Theologica presents justice as giving each person their due, with a strong emphasis on the common good.

Key Church Documents

Vatican II and Gaudium et Spes

The Second Vatican Council (1962-1965) marked a significant development in the Catholic Church's social teachings. Gaudium et Spes (The Pastoral Constitution on the Church in the Modern World) emphasizes the Church's commitment to social justice, the dignity of the human person, and the importance of community.

> "The joys and the hopes, the griefs and the anxieties of the men of this age, especially those who are poor or in any way afflicted, these are the joys and hopes, the griefs and anxieties of the followers of Christ." (Gaudium et Spes, 1)

This document underscores the Church's mission to address social injustices and promote the common good, aligning closely with the principles of restorative justice.

The Catechism of the Catholic Church

The Catechism of the Catholic Church (1992) provides a comprehensive summary of Catholic doctrine, including its teachings on justice.

> "Justice is the moral virtue that consists in the constant and firm will to give their due to God and neighbor." (CCC 1807)

The Catechism outlines the importance of social justice, emphasizing the role of structures and institutions in promoting fairness and addressing inequalities. It also highlights the need for restorative practices that seek to rehabilitate offenders and restore relationships.

Papal Encyclicals

Various papal encyclicals have addressed issues related to justice, providing further insights into the Catholic perspective.

Rerum Novarum (1891)

Pope Leo XIII's Rerum Novarum addresses the conditions of the working class and the rights and duties of workers and employers. It calls for a just social order that respects human dignity and promotes the common good.

Evangelii Gaudium (2013)

Pope Francis, in Evangelii Gaudium, emphasizes the Church's commitment to the poor and marginalized, advocating for a just economic system that includes everyone.

> "The Church, guided by the Gospel of mercy and by love for mankind, hears the cry for justice and intends to respond to it with all her might." (Evangelii Gaudium, 188)

Principles of Catholic Social Teaching

Catholic social teaching provides a framework for understanding and implementing restorative justice through several key principles:

The Dignity of the Human Person

Central to Catholic social teaching is the inherent dignity of every human being, created in the image of God. This principle underlies the Church's approach to justice, emphasizing respect for each person's dignity and the need for restorative practices that heal and rehabilitate rather than merely punish.

The Common Good

The common good refers to the conditions that allow all individuals and communities to reach their fulfillment. Catholic teaching emphasizes that justice must seek to promote the common good, balancing individual rights with the needs of the broader community.

Solidarity

Solidarity is the recognition of our interconnectedness and the commitment to the well-being of others. It calls for a justice that goes beyond individual interests to consider the impact of actions on the entire community, fostering a sense of mutual responsibility and care.

Subsidiarity

Subsidiarity is the principle that decisions should be made at the most local level possible, empowering individuals and communities to take responsibility for their own affairs. In terms of justice, this principle supports restorative practices that involve community-based solutions and local participation in addressing harm and restoring relationships.

Practical Implications and Applications

Restorative Justice in Practice

Catholic organizations and institutions have been at the forefront of implementing restorative justice practices in various settings, including criminal justice, education, and community reconciliation.

Criminal Justice

Catholic advocacy for restorative justice in the criminal justice system emphasizes rehabilitation and reintegration of offenders, support for victims, and community involvement in the justice process. Programs such as victim-offender mediation and restorative circles reflect the Church's commitment to healing and reconciliation.

Education

Catholic schools and universities incorporate restorative justice principles in their disciplinary approaches, focusing on repairing harm, fostering accountability, and building a supportive community environment. This approach aligns with the broader educational mission of forming individuals who are not only academically proficient but also morally and socially responsible.

Community Reconciliation

Catholic initiatives in community reconciliation address conflicts and injustices through dialogue, mediation, and restorative practices. These efforts aim to rebuild trust, restore relationships, and promote peace within communities.

Advocacy and Policy

The Catholic Church actively advocates for policies that reflect restorative justice principles. This includes support for criminal justice reform, initiatives to address social and economic inequalities, and efforts to promote peace and reconciliation in conflict-affected areas.

Criminal Justice Reform

Catholic advocacy for criminal justice reform focuses on humane treatment of prisoners, alternatives to incarceration, and support for restorative justice practices that seek to rehabilitate offenders and repair harm to victims and communities.

Social and Economic Justice

The Church's commitment to social and economic justice includes addressing the root causes of poverty and inequality, advocating for fair wages, and promoting policies that ensure access to essential services such as healthcare and education.

Peace and Reconciliation

Catholic organizations work in conflict zones and post-conflict settings to promote peace and reconciliation. These efforts involve facilitating dialogue between conflicting parties, supporting transitional justice mechanisms, and helping communities rebuild after violence and trauma.

Conclusion

The Catholic view of restorative justice is deeply rooted in its theological, scriptural, and social teachings. By emphasizing the dignity of the human person, the common good, solidarity, and subsidiarity, the Catholic Church advocates for a justice system that heals, reconciles, and restores. Through its teachings, advocacy, and practical initiatives, the Church seeks to transform individuals and communities, embodying the restorative vision of justice that reflects the heart of the gospel. This perspective challenges both individuals and societies to embrace practices that promote healing and reconciliation, ultimately fostering a more just and compassionate world.

Protestant Views on Restorative Justice

Introduction

Protestant Christianity encompasses a wide range of theological traditions and perspectives, from Lutheran and Reformed to Methodist, Baptist, and Pentecostal. Despite this diversity, there are common threads in how these traditions understand and implement restorative justice. This chapter explores the Protestant perspective on restorative justice, examining its biblical foundations, theological principles, historical development, and contemporary applications.

Biblical Foundations

Old Testament Foundations

Protestant views on restorative justice draw heavily on the Old Testament, where justice is portrayed as central to God's character and His covenant with Israel. Key themes include:

Covenantal Justice

Justice in the Old Testament is often linked to God's covenant with Israel. The laws given to Moses emphasize fairness, restitution, and care for the vulnerable. Passages like Micah 6:8 encapsulate the call to act justly, love mercy, and walk humbly with God.

Prophetic Calls for Justice

The prophets, such as Isaiah, Amos, and Micah, frequently called Israel to repent and return to just living. They condemned social injustices and called for the restoration of right relationships. Amos 5:24, "But let justice roll on like a river, righteousness like a never-failing stream," is a hallmark of this prophetic vision.

New Testament Teachings

The New Testament continues and fulfills the Old Testament themes of justice through the teachings of Jesus and the apostles.

Jesus' Ministry

Jesus' teachings in the Sermon on the Mount (Matthew 5-7) and His parables, such as the Good Samaritan (Luke 10:25-37) and the Prodigal Son (Luke 15:11-32), highlight the importance of mercy, forgiveness, and restorative relationships. His actions, like forgiving the woman caught in adultery (John 8:1-11), emphasize restorative over punitive justice.

Pauline Theology

The Apostle Paul's letters also provide a foundation for restorative justice. For instance, in Romans 12:17-21, Paul urges believers not to repay evil for evil but to overcome evil with good. His letter to Philemon is a practical example of advocating for reconciliation and transformation of relationships.

Theological Principles

Justification by Faith

One of the central tenets of Protestant theology is justification by faith alone (sola fide). This principle emphasizes that righteousness is granted by God's grace through faith in Jesus Christ, not by human works. This understanding impacts views on justice, emphasizing God's mercy and grace in restoring sinners.

Priesthood of All Believers

The doctrine of the priesthood of all believers (1 Peter 2:9) underscores the equality of all Christians before God and their shared responsibility in promoting justice. This principle supports a community-based approach to justice, where each member plays a role in reconciliation and restoration.

Sanctification and Ethical Living

Protestant theology places a strong emphasis on sanctification—the process of becoming holy and living out one's faith in practical ways. This includes ethical living, social responsibility, and active pursuit of justice, as reflected in John Wesley's social principles or the Reformed emphasis on cultural mandate.

Historical Development

Reformation Roots

The Protestant Reformation, led by figures like Martin Luther, John Calvin, and Ulrich Zwingli, sought to reform the church and return to biblical principles. This movement emphasized the authority of Scripture and the necessity of faith for salvation, laying a foundation for later Protestant views on justice.

Social Reform Movements

Protestantism has been at the forefront of many social reform movements, advocating for abolition of slavery, civil rights, and social justice. Leaders like William Wilberforce, a devout evangelical Christian, played crucial roles in ending the transatlantic slave trade. Similarly, Martin Luther King Jr., a Baptist minister, championed civil rights and emphasized justice rooted in Christian love and nonviolence.

Modern Developments

Contemporary Protestant denominations continue to engage with restorative justice through various initiatives and theological reflections. These efforts are often informed by historical commitments to social justice and the ongoing interpretation of biblical teachings.

Contemporary Applications

Restorative Practices in Churches

Many Protestant churches have embraced restorative practices within their congregations and communities. These practices include:

Restorative Discipline

Churches often employ restorative discipline methods, focusing on reconciliation and rehabilitation rather than mere punishment. This approach seeks to restore offenders to the community, encouraging repentance and forgiveness.

Victim-Offender Mediation

Some Protestant communities participate in victim-offender mediation programs, where offenders meet with their victims to understand the impact of their actions and work towards making amends. This practice aligns with biblical principles of confession, repentance, and reconciliation.

Advocacy and Social Justice

Protestant denominations actively advocate for restorative justice at the societal level, addressing systemic injustices and promoting policies that reflect Christian ethics.

Criminal Justice Reform

Protestant organizations and leaders often support criminal justice reform initiatives that focus on rehabilitation rather than punitive measures. They advocate for fair sentencing, alternatives to incarceration, and support for reentry programs that help former inmates reintegrate into society.

Social and Economic Justice

Protestants engage in social and economic justice efforts, addressing issues such as poverty, homelessness, and inequality. This work is often inspired by the biblical call to care for the "least of these" (Matthew 25:40).

Peace and Reconciliation

Many Protestant groups are involved in peacebuilding and reconciliation efforts, both locally and globally. This includes initiatives to resolve conflicts, promote healing in post-conflict areas, and foster dialogue between divided communities.

Education and Formation

Protestant educational institutions play a significant role in promoting restorative justice through teaching and research.

Theological Education

Seminaries and theological schools incorporate restorative justice into their curricula, training future pastors and leaders in these principles. Courses on ethics, social justice, and pastoral care emphasize the importance of restorative approaches in ministry.

Community Outreach

Protestant churches and organizations engage in community outreach programs that embody restorative justice principles. This includes providing support for marginalized groups, facilitating community dialogues, and offering services that promote healing and reconciliation.

Case Studies

The Mennonite Central Committee

The Mennonite Central Committee (MCC) is a notable example of a Protestant organization dedicated to restorative justice. Rooted in Anabaptist traditions, the MCC works on peacebuilding, conflict resolution, and restorative justice initiatives worldwide. Their work includes victim-offender reconciliation programs, support for trauma healing, and advocacy for just policies.

Evangelical Advocacy for Prison Reform

Evangelical leaders and organizations have been vocal advocates for prison reform, emphasizing rehabilitation and restorative justice. The Prison Fellowship, founded by Charles Colson, is a key player in this area, offering programs that support inmates, victims, and families, and advocating for criminal justice reforms that promote restorative practices.

Presbyterian Peacemaking Program

The Presbyterian Peacemaking Program, part of the Presbyterian Church (USA), focuses on promoting peace and justice through education, advocacy, and direct action. Their initiatives include conflict resolution, support for victims of violence, and efforts to address systemic injustices.

Conclusion

Protestant views on restorative justice are deeply rooted in biblical teachings, theological principles, and historical commitments to social reform. By emphasizing justification by faith, the priesthood of all believers, and sanctification, Protestants advocate for a justice that is transformative and restorative. Contemporary Protestant denominations continue to engage with restorative justice through church practices, advocacy, education, and global initiatives, seeking to embody the gospel's call to justice, mercy, and reconciliation. This perspective challenges believers to actively participate in the restoration of individuals and communities, reflecting the holistic and redemptive vision of justice presented in Scripture.

Orthodox Views on Restorative Justice

Introduction

The Orthodox Christian tradition, with its rich theological heritage and emphasis on the transformative nature of the divine-human relationship, offers a unique perspective on restorative justice. Rooted in the teachings of the early Church Fathers, liturgical practices, and the sacraments, Orthodox theology emphasizes healing, reconciliation, and the restoration of communion with God and neighbor. This chapter explores the Orthodox understanding of restorative justice, examining its scriptural foundations, theological principles, historical development, and contemporary applications.

Scriptural Foundations

Old Testament Foundations

The Old Testament provides a significant foundation for the Orthodox understanding of justice, emphasizing the themes of mercy, righteousness, and the restoration of relationships.

Prophetic Vision of Justice

The prophets of the Old Testament, such as Isaiah, Jeremiah, and Amos, call for justice that includes caring for the poor, the oppressed, and the marginalized. Their vision is not limited to legal justice but encompasses a holistic restoration of societal relationships.

> "He has shown you, O mortal, what is good. And what does the Lord require of you? To act justly and to love mercy and to walk humbly with your God." (Micah 6:8)

This prophetic call aligns with the Orthodox emphasis on mercy and communal harmony.

New Testament Teachings

The New Testament continues and fulfills Old Testament themes, particularly through the teachings and actions of Jesus Christ.

Jesus' Ministry

Jesus' ministry, as recorded in the Gospels, is central to the Orthodox understanding of restorative justice. His teachings in the Sermon on the Mount (Matthew 5-7), His parables like the Good Samaritan (Luke 10:25-37), and His acts of healing and forgiveness all exemplify restorative justice.

> "Blessed are the merciful, for they will be shown mercy." (Matthew 5:7)

Jesus' emphasis on mercy, forgiveness, and reconciliation is foundational to Orthodox theology.

Pauline Contributions

The Apostle Paul's writings also contribute to the Orthodox perspective on justice. In Romans 12:17-21, Paul exhorts believers to overcome evil with good, highlighting a restorative approach to justice.

> "Do not repay anyone evil for evil. Be careful to do what is right in the eyes of everyone... Do not be overcome by evil, but overcome evil with good." (Romans 12:17, 21)

Theological Principles

Theosis and Transformation

Central to Orthodox theology is the concept of theosis, or deification, which refers to the process of becoming partakers of the divine nature. This transformative process involves the restoration of the image of God in humanity and is closely linked to the idea of restorative justice.

> "God became man so that man might become god." (St. Athanasius, On the Incarnation)

Theosis emphasizes healing and transformation, seeking to restore individuals and communities to their intended state of communion with God.

Sacramental Life

The sacraments, particularly Confession and Eucharist, play a crucial role in the Orthodox understanding of restorative justice.

Confession

The sacrament of Confession, or Reconciliation, is a powerful expression of restorative justice. Through confession and absolution, individuals experience forgiveness, healing, and restoration to the community.

> "If we confess our sins, he is faithful and just to forgive us our sins and to cleanse us from all unrighteousness." (1 John 1:9)

Eucharist

The Eucharist, or Divine Liturgy, is the sacrament of communion and unity. It embodies the reconciliation of humanity with God and with one another, fostering a community of love and justice.

Communal and Personal Responsibility

Orthodox theology emphasizes both communal and personal responsibility in the pursuit of justice. The community is seen as the context in which individuals grow in virtue and holiness, and personal transformation is understood as contributing to the well-being of the entire body of Christ.

Historical Development

Early Church Fathers

The teachings of the early Church Fathers, such as St. Basil the Great, St. John Chrysostom, and St. Gregory the Theologian, provide a foundation for the Orthodox understanding of justice.

St. Basil the Great

St. Basil emphasized social justice and the care of the poor. He established hospitals and social services, advocating for a society that reflects Christian compassion and justice.

> "The bread you store up belongs to the hungry; the cloak that lies in your chest belongs to the naked; and the gold you have hidden in the ground belongs to the poor." (St. Basil the Great)

St. John Chrysostom

St. John Chrysostom, known for his eloquent preaching, often addressed issues of social justice and the ethical responsibilities of Christians.

> "The rich are in possession of the goods of the poor, even if they have acquired them honestly or inherited them legally." (St. John Chrysostom)

Byzantine and Post-Byzantine Periods

Throughout the Byzantine and post-Byzantine periods, the Orthodox Church continued to emphasize justice through charitable works, the establishment of philanthropic institutions, and the promotion of social harmony.

Contemporary Applications

Restorative Practices in the Church

The Orthodox Church implements restorative justice principles within its communities through various practices.

Parish Life

Orthodox parishes often serve as centers for community support and reconciliation. Clergy and lay leaders work together to address conflicts, promote healing, and restore relationships.

Counseling and Spiritual Guidance

Orthodox priests provide counseling and spiritual guidance, helping individuals navigate personal struggles and encouraging them towards repentance and reconciliation.

Advocacy and Social Justice

The Orthodox Church actively engages in social justice advocacy, addressing contemporary issues through the lens of its theological principles.

Human Rights and Dignity

Orthodox organizations advocate for human rights and the dignity of all individuals, reflecting the Church's commitment to justice and mercy.

Peacebuilding and Reconciliation

Orthodox initiatives in peacebuilding and reconciliation seek to address conflicts and promote healing in divided communities. These efforts often involve dialogue, mediation, and support for victims of violence.

Education and Formation

Orthodox educational institutions and programs emphasize the importance of restorative justice in Christian life.

heological Education

Seminaries and theological schools incorporate teachings on justice, mercy, and reconciliation into their curricula, preparing future clergy and lay leaders to embody these principles in their ministries.

Youth and Adult Formation

Programs for youth and adult formation focus on developing a holistic understanding of justice that includes personal virtue, communal responsibility, and social engagement.

Case Studies

St. Basil's Philanthropic Initiatives

St. Basil the Great's establishment of the Basiliad, a complex of charitable institutions including hospitals, hostels, and schools, serves as a historical example of the Orthodox commitment to restorative justice. This initiative provided care and support for the poor, sick, and marginalized, embodying the principles of Christian compassion and justice.

Orthodox Peace Fellowship

The Orthodox Peace Fellowship (OPF) is a contemporary organization dedicated to promoting peace, justice, and reconciliation. OPF members engage in various activities, including advocacy, education, and direct action, to address issues of violence, poverty, and injustice.

Conclusion

The Orthodox Christian perspective on restorative justice is deeply rooted in its theological, liturgical, and communal life. By emphasizing the transformative process of theosis, the sacramental life, and the importance of both personal and communal responsibility, the Orthodox Church offers a comprehensive vision of justice that seeks to heal, reconcile, and restore. Through its historical and contemporary applications, the Orthodox tradition continues to embody the principles of restorative justice, challenging believers to live out their faith in ways that reflect the mercy, love, and justice of God. This perspective calls the faithful to actively participate in the restoration of individuals and communities, fostering a world that reflects the Kingdom of God.

The Role of Forgiveness and Reconciliation in Christian Theology

Introduction

Forgiveness and reconciliation are central tenets of Christian theology, deeply rooted in the teachings of Jesus and the broader biblical narrative. These concepts are not only essential for personal spiritual growth but also for the health and unity of the Christian community. This chapter explores the theological foundations of forgiveness and reconciliation, their significance in Christian doctrine, and their practical implications for individuals and communities.

Theological Foundations

Biblical Basis

Old Testament Foundations

The Old Testament sets the stage for understanding forgiveness and reconciliation through its narratives, laws, and prophetic writings. Key examples include:

- Joseph and His Brothers: The story of Joseph in Genesis 37-50 exemplifies forgiveness and reconciliation. Despite being sold into slavery by his brothers, Joseph forgives them and restores their relationship, recognizing God's providence in his suffering (Genesis 50:19-21).

- Levitical Laws: The Levitical laws emphasize restitution and reconciliation within the community. For example, Leviticus 19:18 commands, "You shall not take vengeance or bear a grudge against the sons of your own people, but you shall love your neighbor as yourself: I am the Lord."

New Testament Teachings

The New Testament, particularly through the teachings of Jesus and the writings of Paul, provides a fuller revelation of forgiveness and reconciliation.

- Jesus' Teachings: Jesus' teachings in the Gospels emphasize the necessity of forgiveness and the process of reconciliation. The Lord's Prayer includes a plea for forgiveness, linking our forgiveness of others with God's forgiveness of us (Matthew 6:12). The parable of the unforgiving servant (Matthew 18:21-35) illustrates the importance of forgiving others as we have been forgiven by God.

- Pauline Theology: The Apostle Paul's letters further develop these themes. In 2 Corinthians 5:18-19, Paul describes the ministry of reconciliation, stating that God reconciled us to Himself through Christ and gave us the ministry of reconciliation. He emphasizes that forgiveness and reconciliation are at the heart of the gospel message.

Doctrinal Significance

Forgiveness and reconciliation are not merely ethical imperatives but are deeply embedded in Christian doctrine.

Atonement and Forgiveness

The doctrine of atonement is central to understanding Christian forgiveness. Through Jesus' sacrificial death and resurrection, believers receive forgiveness of sins and are reconciled to God. This is encapsulated in Ephesians 1:7: "In Him we have redemption through His blood, the forgiveness of sins, in accordance with the riches of God's grace."

Justification and Sanctification

Justification involves being declared righteous before God, while sanctification is the process of becoming holy. Forgiveness is integral to both. Justification includes the forgiveness of sins, while sanctification involves growing in the ability to forgive others and seek reconciliation.

Practical Implications

Personal Spiritual Growth

Forgiveness and reconciliation are vital for personal spiritual health. Harboring unforgiveness and unresolved conflict can hinder one's relationship with God and others. Christians are called to emulate Christ's example of forgiveness, recognizing that forgiving others is a response to God's grace in their own lives.

Healing and Freedom

Forgiveness brings healing and freedom from the burden of resentment and bitterness. It allows individuals to move forward in their spiritual journey and experience the peace of Christ (Colossians 3:13-15).

Obedience to Christ

Forgiving others is an act of obedience to Christ's commands. Jesus taught that forgiveness is essential for maintaining a right relationship with God (Matthew 6:14-15).

Community Life

Forgiveness and reconciliation are also crucial for the unity and health of the Christian community.

Church Discipline and Restoration

Church discipline, when practiced biblically, aims at restoration rather than punishment. Matthew 18:15-17 outlines a process for addressing sin within the community, emphasizing reconciliation and the restoration of relationships.

Promoting Unity

Forgiveness fosters unity within the body of Christ. Paul exhorts believers in Ephesians 4:32 to "be kind and compassionate to one another, forgiving each other, just as in Christ God forgave you." This creates a community marked by love and mutual support.

Witness to the World

Forgiveness and reconciliation also serve as a powerful witness to the world. In a culture often characterized by division and retribution, the Christian practice of forgiveness stands out as a radical testimony to the transforming power of the gospel.

Demonstrating God's Love

By forgiving others, Christians demonstrate the love and mercy of God. This can open doors for evangelism and show non-believers the reality of God's grace.

Building Bridges

Forgiveness and reconciliation can build bridges in divided communities and promote peace. Christians are called to be peacemakers (Matthew 5:9), actively working to reconcile broken relationships and heal societal wounds.

Challenges and Misconceptions

While forgiveness and reconciliation are central to Christian theology, they are not without challenges and misconceptions.

Forgiveness Does Not Mean Excusing Wrongdoing

Forgiveness does not mean excusing or minimizing the wrongdoing. It involves acknowledging the offense and choosing to forgive despite the hurt.

Reconciliation Requires Both Parties

While forgiveness can be extended unilaterally, reconciliation requires the willingness of both parties. It involves rebuilding trust and restoring the relationship, which can be a gradual process.

The Role of Justice

Forgiveness and reconciliation do not negate the need for justice. In fact, true reconciliation often involves addressing the underlying injustices and working towards a fair resolution.

Case Studies

The Amish Community

The Amish community's response to the 2006 school shooting in Nickel Mines, Pennsylvania, is a powerful example of Christian forgiveness. The community forgave the shooter and extended compassion to his family, demonstrating the profound impact of forgiveness and reconciliation.

Truth and Reconciliation Commissions

Truth and Reconciliation Commissions, such as those in South Africa after apartheid, illustrate how Christian principles of forgiveness and reconciliation can be applied on a societal level. These commissions focus on acknowledging past wrongs, promoting forgiveness, and fostering reconciliation to heal divided communities.

Conclusion

Forgiveness and reconciliation are foundational to Christian theology, reflecting the heart of the gospel message. Rooted in the teachings of Jesus and the broader biblical narrative, these concepts emphasize the transformative power of God's grace and the restoration of relationships. In both personal spiritual growth and community life, practicing forgiveness and reconciliation fosters healing, unity, and a powerful witness to the world. Despite the challenges and misconceptions, Christians are called to embody these principles, reflecting the love and mercy of God in their interactions with others. By doing so, they participate in God's redemptive work, promoting a culture of forgiveness and reconciliation that mirrors the Kingdom of God.

CHAPTER 03

HISTORICAL PERSPECTIVES

Historical Practices of Justice and Reconciliation in Early Christianity

Introduction

Justice and reconciliation have been integral aspects of Christian theology and practice since the inception of the Church. The early Christian community inherited and transformed the concepts of justice and reconciliation from their Jewish roots and Greco-Roman context. This chapter explores the historical perspective of justice in early Christianity, the distinctively Christian approach to justice, and the ways in which reconciliation was practiced and emphasized.

1. The Historical Perspective of Justice

Jewish Roots of Justice

Covenantal Justice

The Jewish understanding of justice was deeply rooted in the covenantal relationship between God and Israel. Justice (tzedakah) and righteousness (mishpat) were seen as fundamental aspects of living in accordance with God's will. The Law of Moses provided detailed instructions for maintaining justice in various aspects of life, including economic transactions, social relations, and religious practices.

Prophetic Tradition

The prophets of Israel, such as Isaiah, Amos, and Micah, played a crucial role in calling the people back to covenantal faithfulness. They condemned social injustices, exploitation, and idolatry, emphasizing that true worship of God included practicing justice and showing mercy.

> "But let justice roll on like a river, righteousness like a never-failing stream!" (Amos 5:24)

Greco-Roman Context

Roman Law

The Roman legal system, known for its complexity and structure, influenced the early Christian understanding of justice. Roman law emphasized order, retribution, and the rights of citizens. Concepts such as ius (law) and aequitas (equity) were central to the Roman approach to justice.

Philosophical Influences

Greco-Roman philosophy also shaped the early Christian perspective on justice. Philosophers like Plato and Aristotle discussed justice as a cardinal virtue, essential for the well-being of individuals and society. Stoicism, in particular, emphasized universal reason and natural law, which resonated with early Christian thinkers.

2. Early Christian Perspective on Justice

Teachings of Jesus

Sermon on the Mount

Jesus' teachings, especially the Sermon on the Mount (Matthew 5-7), redefined traditional concepts of justice. He emphasized mercy, forgiveness, and love for enemies, presenting a radical vision of justice that transcended retribution and legalism.

> "Blessed are those who hunger and thirst for righteousness, for they will be filled." (Matthew 5:6)

Parables and Miracles

Jesus' parables, such as the Good Samaritan (Luke 10:25-37) and the Prodigal Son (Luke 15:11-32), illustrated the principles of restorative justice and reconciliation. His miracles of healing and acts of forgiveness further demonstrated the transformative power of divine justice.

Apostolic Teachings

Pauline Theology

The Apostle Paul's writings were foundational for the early Christian understanding of justice. In his letters, Paul emphasized justification by faith and the reconciliation of humanity with God through Christ. He also addressed social justice issues, such as the treatment of slaves and the equality of all believers.

> "There is neither Jew nor Gentile, neither slave nor free, nor is there male and female, for you are all one in Christ Jesus." (Galatians 3:28)

Other Apostolic Writings

The Epistle of James emphasizes practical righteousness and social justice, calling believers to care for the poor and marginalized.

> "Religion that God our Father accepts as pure and faultless is this: to look after orphans and widows in their distress and to keep oneself from being polluted by the world." (James 1:27)

Early Church Practices

Communal Living

The early Christian community in Jerusalem practiced a form of communal living, where believers shared their possessions and ensured that no one was in need.

> "All the believers were together and had everything in common. They sold property and possessions to give to anyone who had need." (Acts 2:44-45)

Charitable Acts

Early Christians were known for their acts of charity and care for the poor, sick, and marginalized. This practice of almsgiving and hospitality was seen as an essential expression of Christian faith and justice.

Reconciliation in the Early Church

Forgiveness and Restoration

The early Church emphasized the importance of forgiveness and reconciliation within the community. Practices such as confession and penance were developed to restore relationships between individuals and between believers and God.

Conflict Resolution

The early Church also established processes for resolving conflicts and disputes among believers. The Council of Jerusalem (Acts 15), for example, addressed the contentious issue of Gentile converts and the requirements of the Mosaic Law, seeking a resolution that promoted unity and inclusivity.

> "It seemed good to the Holy Spirit and to us not to burden you with anything beyond the following requirements..." (Acts 15:28)

3. Reconciliation Between Justice and Forgiveness

Theological Synthesis

Integration of Justice and Mercy

Early Christian theology sought to integrate justice and mercy, reflecting the nature of God as both just and merciful. This synthesis is evident in the doctrine of atonement, where Christ's sacrificial death satisfies divine justice and extends mercy to sinners.

Role of the Church

The Church was seen as the body of Christ, tasked with embodying and promoting justice and reconciliation in the world. This involved both preaching the gospel of forgiveness and engaging in social actions that reflected God's justice.

Practical Outworking

Liturgical Practices

Liturgical practices, such as the Eucharist, embodied the principles of justice and reconciliation. The Eucharist was a sacrament of unity, reminding believers of their reconciliation with God and with each other through Christ's body and blood.

Social and Economic Justice

The early Church's emphasis on caring for the poor and advocating for social justice was a practical outworking of its theology. This included establishing charitable institutions, advocating for the rights of the oppressed, and living out the principles of equity and fairness in everyday life.

Legacy and Influence

Development of Christian Doctrine

The early Church's practices and teachings on justice and reconciliation laid the groundwork for the development of Christian doctrine and social teaching throughout history. This legacy continues to influence contemporary Christian thought and practice.

Influence on Society

The early Christian emphasis on justice and reconciliation had a profound impact on the broader society, contributing to the development of social welfare systems, legal reforms, and ethical standards that promoted the dignity and well-being of all people.

Conclusion

The historical practices of justice and reconciliation in early Christianity reflect a profound integration of theological principles and practical action. Rooted in the teachings of Jesus and the apostles, the early Church developed a distinctive approach to justice that emphasized mercy, forgiveness, and the restoration of relationships. Through communal living, charitable acts, and conflict resolution, early Christians sought to embody the justice and reconciliation of God's kingdom. This legacy continues to inspire and challenge Christians today to pursue justice and reconciliation in their own lives and communities, reflecting the transformative power of the gospel.

Impact of Christian Thought on Legal and Judicial Systems

Introduction

Christian thought has profoundly influenced the development of legal and judicial systems throughout history. From the early Church's moral teachings to the codification of laws in Christian empires and the modern legal principles rooted in Christian ethics, the impact of Christianity on the legal sphere is extensive and enduring. This chapter explores the ways in which Christian thought has shaped legal and judicial systems, providing historical examples and contemporary applications.

Historical Influence of Christian Thought on Legal Systems

The Early Church and Roman Law

Moral and Ethical Foundations

The early Christian community, although initially a minority within the Roman Empire, began to influence Roman legal practices through its emphasis on moral and ethical behavior. Early Christian leaders, such as Paul and the Church Fathers, emphasized justice, mercy, and the intrinsic worth of every individual, which gradually permeated Roman thought.

Constantine and the Christianization of Roman Law

The conversion of Emperor Constantine in the early 4th century marked a significant turning point. Constantine's Edict of Milan (313 AD) granted religious tolerance throughout the empire, leading to a closer integration of Christian principles with Roman law. Subsequently, Christian ethics began to inform legal reforms, such as the prohibition of infanticide and the promotion of more humane treatment of slaves.

Medieval Christendom

Canon Law

During the medieval period, the Church developed its own legal system known as canon law. Canon law governed ecclesiastical matters and provided a framework for moral and ethical conduct within Christendom. It covered areas such as marriage, inheritance, and moral offenses, and it influenced secular law by providing a model for legal codification and judicial procedures.

Influence on Secular Law

The Church's influence extended to secular legal systems as well. Many medieval kings and emperors sought the Church's guidance in matters of justice and governance. For instance, the Magna Carta (1215), which laid the foundation for modern constitutional law, was influenced by Archbishop Stephen Langton and included provisions that reflected Christian principles of justice and fairness.

Reformation and Modern Legal Systems

Protestant Reformation

Reformation and Legal Reforms

The Protestant Reformation in the 16th century, led by figures such as Martin Luther and John Calvin, had a significant impact on legal thought and practice. The reformers emphasized the authority of Scripture and the priesthood of all believers, which contributed to the development of more equitable legal systems. Protestant regions saw the implementation of legal reforms that promoted education, social welfare, and individual rights.

Impact on Western Legal Traditions

The Reformation's emphasis on individual conscience and moral responsibility influenced the development of Western legal traditions, particularly in England and the United States. The principles of natural law, human rights, and the rule of law were underpinned by Protestant ethical teachings and became foundational to modern democratic societies.

Enlightenment and Legal Rationalism

Christian Ethics and Enlightenment Thought

The Enlightenment period saw the emergence of legal rationalism and the development of modern legal systems. While Enlightenment thinkers often critiqued institutional religion, Christian ethics continued to influence legal philosophy. Concepts such as equality before the law, the inherent dignity of the individual, and the importance of justice were rooted in Christian thought and were integral to Enlightenment legal reforms.

Living Exhibit: The Declaration of Independence

The American Declaration of Independence (1776) is a living exhibit of the influence of Christian ethics on modern legal systems. It proclaims that "all men are created equal" and "endowed by their Creator with certain unalienable Rights," reflecting the Christian belief in the inherent dignity and worth of every human being.

Contemporary Influence of Christianity on Legal Systems

Human Rights and Social Justice

Universal Declaration of Human Rights

The Universal Declaration of Human Rights (1948) is another living exhibit of Christian influence. Drafted in the aftermath of World War II, it was significantly shaped by Christian thinkers such as Charles Malik, a Lebanese philosopher and diplomat. The declaration enshrines principles of justice, equality, and human dignity that resonate with Christian teachings.

Advocacy for Social Justice

Contemporary Christian organizations and leaders continue to advocate for social justice and legal reforms. The Catholic Church's social teaching, encapsulated in documents like Rerum Novarum (1891) and Laudato Si' (2015), calls for economic justice, environmental stewardship, and the protection of human rights. Protestant denominations and ecumenical bodies, such as the World Council of Churches, also play a significant role in promoting justice and advocating for the marginalized.

Restorative Justice Practices

Living Exhibit: Restorative Justice Programs

Restorative justice programs, inspired by Christian principles of reconciliation and forgiveness, have been implemented in various legal systems worldwide. These programs focus on healing and restoring relationships rather than simply punishing offenders. They involve victims, offenders, and the community in a process of dialogue, restitution, and rehabilitation.

Example: Truth and Reconciliation Commissions

Truth and Reconciliation Commissions (TRCs), such as those in South Africa and Canada, are living exhibits of restorative justice. These commissions, often supported by Christian leaders, aim to address historical injustices and promote healing and reconciliation within divided societies. The South African TRC, chaired by Archbishop Desmond Tutu, played a crucial role in the country's transition from apartheid to democracy.

Influence on International Law

Christian Contributions to International Law

Christian thought has also influenced the development of international law. The principles of just war, humanitarian intervention, and the protection of non-combatants in armed conflict have roots in Christian ethical teachings. The work of theologians such as Augustine and

Thomas Aquinas laid the groundwork for the modern concept of international law.

Living Exhibit: The Geneva Conventions

The Geneva Conventions (1949) are a living exhibit of Christian influence on international law. These treaties establish standards for the humane treatment of prisoners of war and civilians during armed conflicts. They reflect the Christian commitment to the dignity and worth of every human being, even in times of war.

The Church's Influence on Judicial Systems

Historical Influence on Judicial Practices

Moral and Ethical Guidance

Throughout history, the Church has provided moral and ethical guidance to judicial systems. Bishops and clergy often served as judges and legal advisors, ensuring that Christian principles informed judicial decisions. The Church's emphasis on justice, mercy, and the protection of the vulnerable influenced the development of more humane legal practices.

Establishment of Ecclesiastical Courts

Ecclesiastical courts, established by the Church to handle matters of canon law, played a significant role in shaping judicial practices. These courts dealt with issues such as marriage, inheritance, and moral conduct, providing a model for fair and just legal proceedings.

Contemporary Engagement with Legal Systems

Advocacy and Legal Reform

In contemporary society, the Church continues to engage with legal systems through advocacy and efforts to promote legal reform. Christian organizations lobby for laws that protect human dignity, promote social justice, and ensure the common good. They also provide legal assistance to marginalized and vulnerable populations.

Living Exhibit: Legal Aid and Advocacy Organizations

Organizations such as the International Justice Mission (IJM) are living exhibits of the Church's influence on judicial systems. IJM, a global Christian human rights organization, works to combat human trafficking, forced labor, and other forms of violence. They partner with local authorities to strengthen judicial systems and ensure justice for victims.

Ethical Training for Legal Professionals

Christian institutions provide ethical training for legal professionals, emphasizing the importance of integrity, justice, and compassion in the practice of law. Seminaries and

Christian universities offer courses in legal ethics, helping to shape the values and principles that guide future lawyers, judges, and policymakers.

Conclusion

Christian thought has had a profound and lasting impact on legal and judicial systems throughout history. From the early Church's moral teachings to the integration of Christian principles into Roman and medieval law, and from the influence of the Reformation to the modern advocacy for human rights and social justice, Christianity has shaped the way justice is understood and practiced. Living exhibits such as the Declaration of Independence, the Universal Declaration of Human Rights, restorative justice programs, and the Geneva Conventions demonstrate the enduring relevance of Christian ethics in the legal sphere. The Church's continued engagement with legal systems through advocacy, legal reform, and ethical training underscores its commitment to promoting justice, mercy, and reconciliation in society. As Christians seek to embody these principles, they contribute to the development of legal and judicial systems that reflect the values of the Kingdom of God.

CHAPTER 04

PRACTICAL APPLICATIONS IN MINISTRY

Case Studies of Restorative Justice in Christian Communities

Introduction

Restorative justice, with its focus on healing, reconciliation, and the restoration of relationships, has found practical applications in various Christian communities around the world. This chapter examines several case studies that highlight how restorative justice principles are implemented within Christian contexts, showcasing the transformative power of these practices.

Case Study 1: The Truth and Reconciliation Commission in South Africa

Background

The Truth and Reconciliation Commission (TRC) in South Africa was established in 1995 following the end of apartheid. It aimed to address the human rights violations that occurred under the apartheid regime and promote national healing and reconciliation. Chaired by Archbishop Desmond Tutu, the TRC was deeply influenced by Christian principles of forgiveness, repentance, and reconciliation.

Process and Implementation

Hearings and Testimonies

The TRC conducted public hearings where victims of apartheid-related abuses could share their stories. Perpetrators of violence were also given the opportunity to confess their actions and request amnesty. The hearings were characterized by a profound emphasis on truth-telling, acknowledging the pain and suffering endured by the victims.

Christian Influence

Archbishop Tutu's leadership brought a distinctly Christian perspective to the TRC's work. He emphasized the importance of forgiveness and reconciliation, drawing on Christian teachings to foster an environment where healing could take place.

> "Without forgiveness, there is no future." — Archbishop Desmond Tutu

Outcomes and Impact

The TRC's work had a significant impact on South Africa's journey towards healing and reconciliation. It provided a platform for victims to be heard and validated, while also encouraging perpetrators to take responsibility for their actions. The process highlighted the power of restorative justice in addressing deep societal wounds and promoting a more just and compassionate society.

Case Study 2: Prison Fellowship International's Restorative Justice Programs

Background

Prison Fellowship International (PFI) is a global Christian organization dedicated to prison ministry and criminal justice reform. PFI's restorative justice programs aim to transform the lives of prisoners, victims, and communities through practices rooted in Christian principles of forgiveness, accountability, and reconciliation.

Process and Implementation

Sycamore Tree Project

One of PFI's flagship programs is the Sycamore Tree Project, which brings together victims and offenders to discuss the impact of crime and the possibility of restoration. The program involves a series of facilitated meetings where participants share their experiences, express remorse, and explore ways to make amends.

Christian Influence

The Sycamore Tree Project draws on the biblical story of Zacchaeus (Luke 19:1-10), who, after encountering Jesus, repented and sought to make restitution for his wrongdoings. This narrative serves as a model for the transformative power of repentance and reconciliation.

> "Today salvation has come to this house, because this man, too, is a son of Abraham." – Luke 19:9

Outcomes and Impact

The Sycamore Tree Project has been implemented in various countries, with significant positive outcomes. Participants often report a profound sense of healing and forgiveness, both for victims and offenders. The program has also contributed to reduced recidivism rates among offenders and improved relationships within communities.

Case Study 3: The Mennonite Central Committee's Peacebuilding Initiatives

Background

The Mennonite Central Committee (MCC) is an Anabaptist organization dedicated to relief, development, and peacebuilding. MCC's peacebuilding initiatives incorporate restorative justice principles, seeking to address conflicts and promote reconciliation in communities affected by violence and injustice.

Process and Implementation

Restorative Justice Workshops

MCC conducts restorative justice workshops in various contexts, including schools, prisons, and conflict-affected communities. These workshops educate participants about restorative justice principles and provide practical tools for resolving conflicts and building peace.

Christian Influence

The Anabaptist tradition, with its emphasis on peacemaking and nonviolence, deeply influences MCC's approach to restorative justice. The teachings of Jesus on forgiveness and reconciliation are central to their peacebuilding efforts.

> "Blessed are the peacemakers, for they will be called children of God." – Matthew 5:9

Outcomes and Impact

MCC's restorative justice workshops have had a transformative impact on individuals and communities. In schools, they have helped reduce bullying and improve student relationships. In conflict-affected areas, they have facilitated dialogue and reconciliation, contributing to lasting peace and social cohesion.

Case Study 4: Healing Circles in Indigenous Communities

Background

Many Indigenous communities have long-standing traditions of restorative justice that align closely with Christian principles. Healing circles, for instance, are a practice where community members gather to address conflicts, promote healing, and restore harmony.

Process and Implementation

Healing Circles

Healing circles typically involve a structured process where participants sit in a circle and speak openly about their experiences and feelings. The process is facilitated by a respected community member and often incorporates elements of Indigenous spirituality and Christian teachings.

Christian Influence

In many cases, Christian missionaries and Indigenous Christian leaders have integrated biblical principles of forgiveness and reconciliation into traditional healing practices. This has enriched the restorative process and strengthened the spiritual dimension of healing circles.

> "For where two or three gather in my name, there am I with them." – Matthew 18:20

Outcomes and Impact

Healing circles have been effective in resolving conflicts and promoting healing in Indigenous communities. They provide a safe space for individuals to express their pain, seek forgiveness, and work toward reconciliation. The integration of Christian teachings has enhanced the spiritual depth of these practices, fostering a sense of communal and divine healing.

Case Study 5: The Church of the Brethren's Reconciliation Ministry

Background

The Church of the Brethren, a historic peace church, has a strong commitment to peacebuilding and restorative justice. Their Reconciliation Ministry focuses on addressing conflicts within congregations and communities through restorative practices.

Process and Implementation

Conflict Resolution Programs

The Reconciliation Ministry offers conflict resolution programs that train church leaders and members in restorative justice principles. These programs include mediation, facilitated dialogues, and peacebuilding workshops.

Christian Influence

The Church of the Brethren's emphasis on following the example of Jesus as the Prince of Peace shapes their approach to reconciliation. They draw on biblical teachings to foster a spirit of humility, forgiveness, and mutual respect.

> "If it is possible, as far as it depends on you, live at peace with everyone." – Romans 12:18

Outcomes and Impact

The Reconciliation Ministry has successfully resolved numerous conflicts within congregations and communities. Participants often report a renewed sense of unity and spiritual growth. The ministry's work has also inspired broader peacebuilding efforts within the denomination and beyond.

Conclusion

These case studies demonstrate the profound impact of restorative justice practices within Christian communities. Rooted in biblical principles and influenced by the teachings of Jesus, these initiatives highlight the transformative power of forgiveness, reconciliation, and healing. From the Truth and Reconciliation Commission in South Africa to the peacebuilding efforts of the Mennonite Central Committee and the Reconciliation Ministry of the Church of the Brethren, Christian communities are actively embodying the principles of restorative justice. These examples serve as powerful testimonies to the potential of restorative justice to heal wounds, restore relationships, and build more just and compassionate societies. As Christians continue to engage with these practices, they bear witness to the redemptive power of the gospel and contribute to the realization of God's kingdom on earth.

The Role of Churches in Promoting Reconciliation

Introduction

Churches play a crucial role in promoting reconciliation, both within their congregations and in the broader community. Grounded in biblical teachings and the example of Jesus Christ, churches are uniquely positioned to facilitate healing, forgiveness, and the restoration of relationships. This chapter explores how churches actively engage in reconciliation efforts and provides living exhibits that illustrate these practices in action.

Biblical Foundations for Reconciliation

Teachings of Jesus

The ministry of Jesus Christ emphasizes reconciliation and forgiveness as central to the Christian faith. Jesus' teachings, particularly in the Sermon on the Mount, highlight the importance of making peace with others:

> "Blessed are the peacemakers, for they will be called children of God." (Matthew 5:9)

The Ministry of Paul

The Apostle Paul also stresses reconciliation in his letters, viewing it as integral to the gospel message. He encourages believers to live in harmony and resolve conflicts through love and mutual respect:

> "All this is from God, who reconciled us to himself through Christ and gave us the ministry of reconciliation." (2 Corinthians 5:18)

Churches as Agents of Reconciliation

Facilitating Forgiveness and Healing

Confession and Penance

Many churches offer the sacrament of confession, where individuals confess their sins and seek forgiveness. This practice provides a structured process for acknowledging wrongdoing, receiving absolution, and being reconciled with God and the community.

Living Exhibit: Catholic Confession and Reconciliation

In the Catholic Church, the sacrament of reconciliation (confession) is a vital practice. Priests provide spiritual guidance and absolution, helping individuals find peace and restoration. This sacrament fosters personal healing and communal harmony, reinforcing the importance of forgiveness.

Support Groups and Counseling

Churches often facilitate support groups and counseling services for those struggling with personal and relational issues. These services offer a safe space for individuals to share their experiences, seek forgiveness, and work toward reconciliation.

Living Exhibit: Celebrate Recovery

Celebrate Recovery is a Christ-centered recovery program found in many churches worldwide. It addresses a wide range of hurts, habits, and hang-ups, promoting healing through the principles of the Beatitudes. The program's emphasis on forgiveness and reconciliation helps participants restore their relationships with God, themselves, and others.

Mediating Conflicts

Conflict Resolution Programs

Churches often serve as mediators in conflicts within their congregations and communities. They offer conflict resolution programs that provide tools and strategies for resolving disputes in a constructive and peaceful manner.

Living Exhibit: Peacemakers Ministries

Peacemakers Ministries offers conflict resolution training and resources based on biblical principles. Their programs equip church leaders and members to address conflicts effectively, fostering a culture of peace and reconciliation within the church and beyond.

Restorative Circles and Dialogues

Restorative circles and dialogues are facilitated meetings where individuals involved in a conflict come together to discuss their issues openly and work toward a resolution. These practices emphasize listening, understanding, and mutual respect.

Living Exhibit: Restorative Circles in the Anglican Church

Some Anglican churches use restorative circles to address conflicts within their congregations. These circles create a space for honest communication and collective problem-solving, helping to restore relationships and build a stronger community.

Advocating for Social Justice

Engaging in Social Justice Initiatives

Churches are often at the forefront of social justice advocacy, addressing systemic issues that contribute to conflict and division. They work to promote equality, human rights, and the well-being of all individuals.

Living Exhibit: The United Methodist Church's Social Principles

The United Methodist Church (UMC) is actively involved in social justice initiatives. Their Social Principles outline the church's commitment to human dignity, environmental stewardship, and economic justice. The UMC's advocacy efforts include campaigns against human trafficking, support for immigrants, and initiatives to reduce poverty.

Promoting Racial Reconciliation

Many churches are engaged in efforts to promote racial reconciliation, addressing historical and ongoing injustices related to race. These initiatives often involve education, dialogue, and collaborative action to build more inclusive communities.

Living Exhibit: The Evangelical Lutheran Church in America's Racial Justice Network

The Evangelical Lutheran Church in America (ELCA) has established a Racial Justice Network to promote racial reconciliation and justice. This network provides resources, training, and support for congregations working to address racial issues and foster inclusive communities.

Building Interfaith and Ecumenical Relationships

Fostering Interfaith Dialogue

Churches often engage in interfaith dialogue to build bridges with other religious communities. These efforts promote mutual understanding, respect, and collaboration on shared concerns.

Living Exhibit: The Interfaith Council of Metropolitan Washington

The Interfaith Council of Metropolitan Washington (IFCMW) brings together representatives from various religious traditions to promote dialogue and cooperation. Through events, educational programs, and joint service projects, IFCMW fosters reconciliation and peace among diverse faith communities.

Promoting Christian Unity

Ecumenical initiatives aim to foster unity among different Christian denominations. By emphasizing shared beliefs and working together on common goals, churches can overcome divisions and build a more united Christian witness.

Living Exhibit: The World Council of Churches

The World Council of Churches (WCC) is an ecumenical organization that promotes Christian unity and collaboration. Through dialogues, joint initiatives, and theological reflections, the WCC works to reconcile differences and strengthen the global Christian community.

Challenges and Opportunities

Addressing Deep-Seated Conflicts

Promoting reconciliation can be challenging, especially when dealing with deep-seated conflicts and historical injustices. Churches must navigate these complexities with sensitivity, patience, and a commitment to justice and healing.

Leveraging Christian Teachings

Christian teachings on forgiveness, mercy, and reconciliation provide powerful tools for addressing conflicts. Churches can leverage these teachings to inspire and guide their reconciliation efforts.

Engaging the Broader Community

Churches have the opportunity to extend their reconciliation efforts beyond their congregations. By partnering with community organizations, government agencies, and other faith groups, churches can amplify their impact and contribute to broader societal healing.

Conclusion

Churches play a vital role in promoting reconciliation, drawing on their rich theological heritage and practical experience to facilitate healing and restoration. Through practices such as confession, counseling, conflict resolution, social justice advocacy, and interfaith dialogue, churches actively work to reconcile individuals and communities. Living exhibits like Celebrate Recovery, Peacemakers Ministries, and the World Council of Churches demonstrate the transformative power of these efforts. As churches continue to engage in reconciliation, they bear witness to the redemptive power of the gospel and contribute to the building of more just, peaceful, and compassionate societies.

CHAPTER 05

ETHICAL CONSIDERATIONS

Ethical Dilemmas in Implementing Restorative Justice

Introduction

Restorative justice, with its focus on healing, reconciliation, and the restoration of relationships, presents a transformative approach to addressing harm and resolving conflicts. However, its implementation raises several ethical dilemmas that need careful consideration. This chapter explores these ethical challenges, examining how they arise and offering insights into how they might be navigated within Christian communities and broader societal contexts.

Ethical Dilemmas in Restorative Justice

Balancing Justice and Mercy

One of the primary ethical dilemmas in restorative justice is finding the right balance between justice and mercy. Restorative justice seeks to emphasize healing and reconciliation, but this can sometimes appear to be at odds with the need for accountability and justice for the victim.

Justice for Victims

Ensuring that victims feel that justice has been served is crucial. Victims need to see that the harm done to them is acknowledged and that the offender is held accountable. However, the restorative approach often focuses on rehabilitation and reconciliation, which might be perceived as too lenient.

Mercy for Offenders

Restorative justice promotes compassion and offers opportunities for offenders to make amends and reintegrate into the community. While this can lead to genuine transformation, it raises the ethical question of whether it adequately addresses the need for punitive measures in cases of severe harm.

Navigating the Dilemma

Balancing these concerns requires a nuanced approach that considers the needs and perspectives of both victims and offenders. Restorative justice practices should ensure that victims have a voice in the process and that offenders genuinely take responsibility for their actions.

Voluntariness and Coercion

Another ethical dilemma involves ensuring that participation in restorative justice processes is truly voluntary. The success of restorative justice relies on the willing participation of all parties, but there can be implicit or explicit pressures that undermine this voluntariness.

Voluntary Participation

For restorative justice to be effective, all participants must engage willingly and openly. This voluntary participation is essential for fostering genuine dialogue and reconciliation.

Risk of Coercion

There is a risk that individuals might feel coerced into participating, whether due to social pressures, legal mandates, or a desire to avoid harsher penalties. This coercion can undermine the integrity of the restorative process and lead to superficial or insincere outcomes.

Ensuring Genuine Consent

To address this dilemma, it is important to create an environment where participants feel free to express their true willingness or reluctance to engage in restorative justice. Clear communication about the voluntary nature of the process and providing alternatives can help mitigate coercion.

Confidentiality and Transparency

Restorative justice processes often involve sensitive and personal information, raising ethical concerns about confidentiality and transparency.

Confidentiality Concerns

Participants need to feel safe sharing their experiences and emotions, knowing that their disclosures will be kept confidential. Breaches of confidentiality can harm relationships and trust within the community.

Need for Transparency

At the same time, there is a need for transparency to ensure accountability and to maintain public trust in the restorative justice process. This transparency is particularly important in cases involving public figures or systemic issues.

Balancing Privacy and Public Interest

Navigating this dilemma involves establishing clear guidelines for confidentiality while also ensuring that the process is transparent enough to maintain credibility and accountability. Participants should be informed about how their information will be used and protected.

Power Imbalances

Power imbalances between participants can pose significant ethical challenges in restorative justice processes.

These imbalances can influence the dynamics of the dialogue and affect the fairness of the outcomes.

Recognizing Power Dynamics

Power imbalances can exist due to various factors, including social status, economic disparity, or personal influence. These dynamics can affect how freely participants feel they can speak and how the process unfolds.

Addressing Power Imbalances

It is essential to acknowledge and address these imbalances to ensure that all participants have an equal opportunity to contribute. Facilitators must be trained to recognize and mitigate power dynamics, creating a more equitable environment for dialogue and reconciliation.

Ensuring Fair Participation

Providing additional support to those with less power, such as legal representation or advocacy, can help level the playing field and ensure that the restorative justice process is fair and inclusive.

Potential for Re-traumatization

Engaging in restorative justice can be a deeply emotional experience, and there is a risk that participants, particularly victims, may be re-traumatized by revisiting the harm they experienced.

Emotional Risks for Victims

Victims may feel vulnerable and exposed when sharing their stories, which can trigger emotional distress and re-traumatization. It is crucial to handle these situations with sensitivity and care.

Support for Offenders

Offenders may also experience emotional challenges as they confront the impact of their actions and seek to make amends. Providing appropriate support for both victims and offenders is essential to prevent further harm.

Creating a Safe Environment

To mitigate these risks, it is important to create a supportive environment where participants feel safe and respected. Access to counseling and psychological support should be available to help participants navigate the emotional aspects of the restorative process.

Cultural Sensitivity and Inclusivity

Restorative justice practices must be culturally sensitive and inclusive, recognizing and respecting the diverse backgrounds and experiences of participants.

Cultural Awareness

Different cultural contexts have varying understandings of justice, reconciliation, and appropriate responses to harm. It is important to be aware of these differences and to adapt restorative practices accordingly.

Inclusivity

Ensuring that restorative justice processes are inclusive involves actively engaging with and respecting the cultural norms and values of all participants. This inclusivity helps to build trust and foster genuine reconciliation.

Adapting Practices

Adapting restorative justice practices to fit the cultural context can enhance their effectiveness and ensure that they are meaningful and respectful for all participants. Involving community leaders and cultural experts can provide valuable insights and guidance.

Living Exhibits of Ethical Considerations in Restorative Justice

Case Study: Truth and Reconciliation Commission in Canada

Background

The Truth and Reconciliation Commission (TRC) in Canada was established to address the legacy of residential schools, where Indigenous children were forcibly removed from their families and subjected to abuse and cultural assimilation.

Ethical Challenges

The TRC faced several ethical dilemmas, including balancing the need for public acknowledgment of the harm done with the confidentiality and safety of survivors. Addressing power imbalances between the government, the church, and Indigenous communities was also crucial.

Approach

The TRC adopted a culturally sensitive approach, involving Indigenous leaders and respecting Indigenous traditions. Confidentiality measures were put in place to protect survivors, while public hearings ensured transparency and accountability.

Impact

The TRC's work has led to greater awareness of the injustices faced by Indigenous peoples and has laid the groundwork for ongoing reconciliation efforts. The ethical considerations addressed by the TRC have provided valuable lessons for future restorative justice initiatives.

Case Study: Restorative Justice Programs in New Zealand

Background

New Zealand has integrated restorative justice into its criminal justice system, particularly for juvenile offenders. These programs involve victims, offenders, and their families in facilitated meetings to discuss the harm caused and agree on a plan for restitution.

Ethical Challenges

Ensuring voluntary participation and addressing power imbalances between young offenders and adult victims posed significant challenges. Additionally, balancing confidentiality with the need for transparency was crucial.

Approach

New Zealand's restorative justice programs prioritize voluntariness, with participants clearly informed about their rights and options. Trained facilitators work to create a supportive and equitable environment. Confidentiality is maintained, but outcomes are monitored to ensure accountability.

Impact

These programs have shown positive results, with high levels of victim satisfaction and reduced recidivism rates among offenders. The ethical considerations addressed in these programs highlight the importance of careful planning and execution in restorative justice initiatives.

Conclusion

Implementing restorative justice involves navigating a range of ethical dilemmas, from balancing justice and mercy to ensuring voluntary participation and addressing power imbalances. By recognizing and addressing these challenges, restorative justice can be a powerful tool for healing, reconciliation, and the restoration of relationships. The case studies from Canada and New Zealand illustrate how these ethical considerations can be effectively managed, providing valuable insights for future restorative justice efforts. As churches and communities continue to embrace restorative justice, they must remain vigilant in upholding ethical standards that honor the dignity and well-being of all participants, reflecting the transformative power of the gospel in their practices.

Challenges and Criticisms from Christian Perspectives

Introduction

While restorative justice is widely regarded as a valuable approach to conflict resolution and healing, it is not without its challenges and criticisms, particularly from within Christian communities. This chapter explores these challenges and offers suggestions for resolving them, drawing on Christian teachings and practices to strengthen the implementation of restorative justice.

Challenges from Christian Perspectives

1. Perceived Leniency

Challenge:

One of the primary criticisms of restorative justice is that it can be perceived as too lenient on offenders. Critics argue that focusing on reconciliation and rehabilitation might downplay the seriousness of the offense and fail to deliver appropriate consequences for wrongdoing.

Suggestions for Resolution:

Emphasize Accountability:

Restorative justice should emphasize accountability and responsibility. Offenders must acknowledge the harm they have caused and take concrete steps to make amends. This can include restitution, community service, or other actions that demonstrate genuine remorse and commitment to change.

Integrate Restorative and Retributive Elements:

Combining restorative and retributive elements can address concerns about leniency. While restorative justice focuses on healing and reconciliation, incorporating appropriate punitive measures can ensure that justice is seen to be served.

Educate Communities:

Education is key to addressing misconceptions about restorative justice. Churches and Christian organizations can provide resources and training to help communities understand the principles and benefits of restorative justice, highlighting its potential for transformative justice that goes beyond mere punishment.

2. Balancing Forgiveness and Justice

Challenge:

Balancing the Christian call to forgiveness with the need for justice can be challenging. Forgiveness is a core Christian value, but it should not negate the need for justice and accountability, particularly in cases of serious harm.

Suggestions for Resolution:

Theological Education:

Churches can provide theological education on the concepts of forgiveness and justice, emphasizing that forgiveness does not mean excusing wrongdoing or avoiding accountability. Instead, it involves a commitment to restorative practices that seek to repair harm and restore relationships.

Support for Victims:

Ensuring that victims receive adequate support and that their voices are heard is crucial. This includes offering pastoral care, counseling, and practical assistance to help victims heal and feel that justice has been done.

Structured Processes:

Implementing structured restorative justice processes that include clear guidelines for accountability can help balance forgiveness with justice. This ensures that forgiveness is accompanied by genuine efforts to make amends and prevent future harm.

3. Power Imbalances

Challenge:

Power imbalances between victims and offenders can complicate the restorative justice process. These imbalances can affect the dynamics of reconciliation efforts and may lead to outcomes that do not fully address the needs of all parties involved.

Suggestions for Resolution:

Trained Facilitators:

Utilizing trained facilitators who are skilled in recognizing and addressing power imbalances can help create a more equitable process. Facilitators can ensure that all participants have an equal opportunity to express their perspectives and that the process is fair and just.

Advocacy and Support:

Providing advocacy and support for those with less power can help level the playing field. This might include legal representation, counseling, or the presence of a trusted advocate during restorative justice meetings.

Inclusive Practices:

Adopting inclusive practices that actively engage all participants and address their specific needs can mitigate power imbalances. This might involve adjusting the process to ensure accessibility and cultural sensitivity.

4. Risk of Re-Traumatization

Challenge:

Engaging in restorative justice processes can be emotionally challenging, particularly for victims who may be re-traumatized by revisiting the harm they experienced.

Suggestions for Resolution:

Create Safe Spaces:

Creating a safe and supportive environment is essential. This includes providing emotional and psychological support, ensuring confidentiality, and allowing participants to set boundaries for what they are comfortable discussing.

Voluntary Participation:

Ensuring that participation is truly voluntary can help prevent re-traumatization. Participants should feel free to opt out or take a break if the process becomes too overwhelming.

Professional Support:

Access to professional support, such as counselors or therapists, can help participants navigate the emotional aspects of restorative justice. Providing these resources can assist in managing trauma and promoting healing.

5. Theological and Doctrinal Differences

Challenge:

Theological and doctrinal differences within Christian communities can pose challenges to implementing restorative justice. Different interpretations of justice, forgiveness, and reconciliation can lead to varying approaches and expectations.

Suggestions for Resolution:

Ecumenical Dialogue:

Encouraging ecumenical dialogue can help bridge theological and doctrinal differences. Churches and Christian organizations can collaborate on restorative justice initiatives, sharing insights and practices that align with their shared values.

Unified Frameworks:

Developing unified frameworks that incorporate diverse theological perspectives can provide a common ground for implementing restorative justice. These frameworks should respect doctrinal differences while emphasizing shared principles of justice and reconciliation.

Ongoing Education:

Ongoing education on restorative justice from a variety of theological perspectives can help foster understanding and cooperation. Churches can offer workshops, seminars, and study groups to explore how restorative justice aligns with their faith traditions.

6. Integration into Existing Legal Systems

Challenge:

Integrating restorative justice into existing legal systems can be complex. There may be resistance from legal authorities or logistical challenges in implementing restorative practices within a predominantly retributive justice framework.

Suggestions for Resolution:

Collaborative Partnerships:

Building collaborative partnerships with legal authorities can facilitate the integration of restorative justice into the existing legal system. Churches and Christian organizations can advocate for restorative practices and work with legal professionals to develop pilot programs and initiatives.

Policy Advocacy:

Engaging in policy advocacy can help promote restorative justice at the legislative level. Christian organizations can lobby for laws and policies that support the use of restorative practices in criminal justice and other areas.

Pilot Programs:

Implementing pilot programs can demonstrate the effectiveness of restorative justice and build support for its broader adoption. These programs can provide valuable data and success stories that highlight the benefits of restorative approaches.

Conclusion

Implementing restorative justice within Christian communities presents several challenges, including balancing justice and mercy, addressing power imbalances, and navigating theological differences. However, by drawing on Christian teachings and practices, these challenges can be effectively addressed. Through theological education, structured processes, trained facilitators, and collaborative partnerships, churches can promote restorative justice in a way that honors the dignity and well-being of all participants. By doing so, they reflect the transformative power of the gospel and contribute to a more just and compassionate society.

CHAPTER 06

CONTEMPORARY ISSUES AND DEBATES

Current Trends and Developments in Christian Views on Restorative Justice

Introduction

In recent years, there has been a growing interest in and application of restorative justice within Christian communities. This trend reflects a broader movement towards embracing principles of healing, reconciliation, and holistic justice in response to harm and conflict. This chapter explores contemporary issues and debates surrounding restorative justice in Christian contexts, highlighting current trends and developments that shape this evolving field.

Increasing Integration of Restorative Practices

Expansion in Church Ministries

Restorative Justice in Congregations

Many churches are increasingly incorporating restorative justice practices into their ministries. This includes using restorative circles for conflict resolution, offering support groups for victims and offenders, and facilitating reconciliation processes within congregations.

Living Exhibit: Restorative Circles at Grace Episcopal Church

Grace Episcopal Church has implemented restorative circles as a regular practice to address conflicts within the congregation. These circles provide a structured space for open dialogue, allowing members to share their experiences, express their feelings, and work toward mutual understanding and resolution.

Integration into Youth Programs

Churches are also integrating restorative justice into youth programs to address issues such as bullying, behavioral problems, and peer conflicts. These programs aim to teach young people principles of accountability, empathy, and reconciliation.

Living Exhibit: Youth Restorative Programs in the United Methodist Church

The United Methodist Church has developed youth restorative programs that focus on building a culture of respect and responsibility. Through workshops, role-playing activities, and peer mediation, young participants learn to resolve conflicts constructively and restore relationships.

Collaboration with Legal Systems

Partnerships with Criminal Justice Systems

There is a growing trend of churches collaborating with legal systems to implement restorative justice programs. These partnerships often involve providing support for victims, facilitating offender rehabilitation, and promoting community-based restorative practices.

Living Exhibit: Faith-Based Restorative Justice Initiatives in the UK

In the United Kingdom, several churches have partnered with the criminal justice system to offer restorative justice programs for offenders. These initiatives include restorative mediation sessions, community service projects, and support groups aimed at reducing recidivism and fostering reconciliation.

Advocacy for Policy Changes

Christian organizations are increasingly advocating for policy changes that support restorative justice. This includes lobbying for legislative reforms, promoting restorative justice education for legal professionals, and raising public awareness about the benefits of restorative approaches.

Living Exhibit: Prison Fellowship International's Advocacy Efforts

Prison Fellowship International has been at the forefront of advocating for restorative justice policies worldwide. Their efforts include engaging with policymakers, conducting research, and organizing conferences to promote restorative justice as a viable alternative to traditional punitive systems.

Emphasis on Trauma-Informed Practices

Addressing Trauma in Restorative Processes

Incorporating Trauma Awareness

A significant trend in contemporary restorative justice is the incorporation of trauma-informed practices. Recognizing the impact of trauma on victims, offenders, and communities, restorative justice practitioners are adopting approaches that prioritize safety, empathy, and healing.

Living Exhibit: Trauma-Informed Restorative Justice Training

Several Christian organizations now offer training on trauma-informed restorative justice. These programs equip facilitators with the skills to recognize and address trauma, ensuring that restorative processes are sensitive to the needs of all participants.

Providing Emotional and Psychological Support

Churches are increasingly providing emotional and psychological support as part of their restorative justice initiatives. This includes offering counseling services, creating support groups, and collaborating with mental health professionals.

Living Exhibit: Counseling Services at St. Mary's Catholic Church

St. Mary's Catholic Church has integrated counseling services into its restorative justice programs. By partnering with local therapists, the church offers comprehensive support for individuals navigating the emotional challenges of the restorative process.

Fostering Resilience and Empowerment

Building Resilience in Communities

Restorative justice programs are also focusing on building resilience in communities affected by conflict and harm. This involves strengthening social networks, promoting positive coping strategies, and empowering individuals to contribute to community healing.

Living Exhibit: Community Resilience Projects in Mennonite Communities

Mennonite communities have developed resilience projects that combine restorative justice with community development. These projects include training in conflict resolution, community-building activities, and initiatives to address social and economic inequalities.

Engagement with Social Justice Movements

Addressing Systemic Injustices

Intersection with Social Justice Issues

Contemporary restorative justice initiatives are increasingly intersecting with broader social justice movements. Churches are addressing systemic injustices such as racial discrimination, economic inequality, and environmental degradation through restorative practices.

Living Exhibit: Racial Reconciliation Programs in the Episcopal Church

The Episcopal Church has launched racial reconciliation programs that use restorative justice principles to address the legacy of racism. These programs involve facilitated dialogues, educational workshops, and community actions aimed at promoting racial healing and justice.

Environmental Restorative Justice

Some Christian communities are exploring the application of restorative justice to environmental issues. This involves addressing the harm caused by environmental degradation and promoting practices that restore ecological balance.

Living Exhibit: Eco-Restorative Initiatives in the Evangelical Lutheran Church in America

The Evangelical Lutheran Church in America has initiated eco-restorative programs that combine environmental stewardship with restorative justice. These initiatives include community clean-up projects, reforestation efforts, and educational campaigns on sustainable living.

Promoting Inclusive and Equitable Practices

Ensuring Inclusivity in Restorative Processes

A key trend is the emphasis on inclusivity and equity in restorative justice practices. Churches are working to ensure that restorative processes are accessible and fair for all participants, regardless of their background or circumstances.

Living Exhibit: Inclusive Restorative Practices in the Church of Scotland

The Church of Scotland has implemented inclusive restorative practices that actively engage marginalized groups. These practices include providing interpretation services, addressing cultural sensitivities, and ensuring that all voices are heard in the restorative process.

Fostering Global Solidarity

Christian communities are also fostering global solidarity through restorative justice. This involves supporting restorative initiatives in different parts of the world and sharing resources and expertise to promote peace and reconciliation globally.

Living Exhibit: Global Restorative Justice Network

The Global Restorative Justice Network, supported by various Christian organizations, facilitates international collaboration on restorative justice. This network connects practitioners, researchers, and advocates, promoting the exchange of knowledge and best practices across borders.

Theological Reflection and Education

Deepening Theological Understanding

Theological Exploration of Restorative Justice

There is a growing emphasis on deepening the theological understanding of restorative justice within Christian communities. This involves exploring biblical teachings, historical traditions, and contemporary theological reflections on justice, forgiveness, and reconciliation.

Living Exhibit: Restorative Justice Seminars at Fuller Theological Seminary

Fuller Theological Seminary offers seminars and courses on restorative justice, integrating theological reflection with practical training. These programs engage students in exploring the theological foundations of restorative justice and its application in various contexts.

Developing Theological Resources

Churches and Christian organizations are developing theological resources that support restorative justice practices. These resources include books, articles, study guides, and liturgical materials that help communities engage with restorative justice from a faith-based perspective.

Living Exhibit: Theological Publications by The Anabaptist Network

The Anabaptist Network publishes theological resources on restorative justice, drawing on the rich Anabaptist tradition of peacemaking and reconciliation. These publications provide theological insights and practical guidance for implementing restorative justice in Christian communities.

Educating and Training Leaders

Training Clergy and Lay Leaders

Educating and training clergy and lay leaders in restorative justice is essential for its effective implementation. Churches are investing in leadership development programs that equip leaders with the knowledge and skills to facilitate restorative processes.

Living Exhibit: Restorative Justice Training by the United Church of Canada

The United Church of Canada offers restorative justice training for clergy and lay leaders, focusing on practical skills such as mediation, conflict resolution, and trauma-informed care. These training programs prepare leaders to implement restorative justice initiatives within their congregations and communities.

Promoting Lifelong Learning

Promoting lifelong learning about restorative justice is another important trend. Churches encourage ongoing education and professional development for those involved in restorative justice, ensuring that they stay informed about best practices and emerging trends.

Living Exhibit: Continuing Education Programs at Wheaton College

Wheaton College offers continuing education programs in restorative justice, providing opportunities for practitioners to deepen their knowledge and skills. These programs include workshops, conferences, and online courses that support lifelong learning and professional growth.

Conclusion

Contemporary trends in Christian views on restorative justice reflect a dynamic and evolving field that integrates theological reflection, practical application, and engagement with broader social justice movements. Churches are increasingly incorporating restorative practices into their ministries, collaborating with legal systems, and addressing systemic injustices. By emphasizing trauma-informed practices, promoting inclusivity, and fostering global solidarity, Christian communities are actively contributing to the development of restorative justice. Through theological education and leadership training, they are equipping the next generation of leaders to continue this important work. These trends demonstrate the ongoing commitment of Christian communities to promoting healing, reconciliation, and holistic justice in response to harm and conflict.

Intersection with Social Justice Movements

Introduction

Restorative justice, with its focus on healing and reconciliation, naturally intersects with broader social justice movements that seek to address systemic inequalities and injustices. This chapter explores how Christian communities are integrating restorative justice with social justice efforts, highlighting the synergies between these approaches and the impact of their combined efforts on society.

Addressing Systemic Injustices

Racial Reconciliation

Historical Context

The legacy of racism and racial discrimination has left deep scars on societies around the world. Christian communities are increasingly recognizing the need to address these issues through both restorative justice and social justice lenses.

Restorative Approaches

Restorative justice offers a way to address the harms caused by racism by focusing on dialogue, understanding, and the rebuilding of relationships. Churches are hosting truth and reconciliation commissions, racial justice workshops, and community dialogues to facilitate healing and promote racial equity.

Living Exhibit: The Episcopal Church's Racial Reconciliation Initiatives

The Episcopal Church has launched a series of racial reconciliation initiatives, including the "Becoming Beloved Community" framework. This initiative encourages congregations to engage in restorative practices such as listening sessions, historical audits, and public witness events to address racial injustices and foster reconciliation.

Economic Justice

Addressing Poverty and Inequality

Economic disparities are a major source of social injustice. Christian communities are using restorative justice principles to address issues of poverty and economic inequality, advocating for fair wages, access to resources, and economic empowerment.

Restorative Practices

Churches are implementing restorative practices that support economic justice, such as community development programs, financial literacy workshops, and support for micro-enterprises. These initiatives aim to create sustainable economic opportunities and address the root causes of poverty.

Living Exhibit: The United Methodist Church's Economic Justice Programs

The United Methodist Church (UMC) has developed economic justice programs that integrate restorative justice principles. These programs include job training initiatives, small business support, and advocacy for economic policies that promote equity and fairness. The UMC's approach emphasizes empowering individuals and communities to achieve economic self-sufficiency.

Environmental Justice

Ecological Stewardship

Environmental degradation disproportionately affects marginalized communities, making environmental justice a critical area of concern. Christian communities are recognizing their role in promoting ecological stewardship and addressing the injustices caused by environmental harm.

Restorative Environmental Practices

Restorative justice approaches to environmental issues involve repairing the damage done to ecosystems and communities. This includes initiatives such as reforestation projects, clean-up campaigns, and advocacy for sustainable practices.

Living Exhibit: The Evangelical Lutheran Church in America's Eco-Restorative Programs

The Evangelical Lutheran Church in America (ELCA) has initiated eco-restorative programs that combine environmental stewardship with restorative justice. These programs include community gardening projects, efforts to reduce carbon footprints, and educational campaigns on ecological responsibility.

Promoting Inclusive and Equitable Practices

Gender Justice

Addressing Gender Inequality

Gender inequality remains a pervasive issue globally. Christian communities are integrating restorative justice principles to address gender-based discrimination and violence, promoting gender equity and empowerment.

Restorative Practices

Restorative justice practices in the context of gender justice include support groups for survivors of gender-based violence, educational programs on gender equality, and advocacy for policies that protect women's rights.

Living Exhibit: The World Council of Churches' Gender Justice Programs

The World Council of Churches (WCC) has implemented gender justice programs that incorporate restorative justice principles. These programs provide safe spaces for dialogue, support for survivors, and advocacy for gender-inclusive policies. The WCC's initiatives aim to create a more just and equitable society for all genders.

Disability Justice

Supporting People with Disabilities

Disability justice focuses on addressing the systemic barriers and discrimination faced by people with disabilities. Christian communities are working to ensure that restorative justice practices are inclusive and accessible to all individuals, regardless of their abilities.

Restorative Practices

Restorative justice practices in disability justice involve creating accessible environments, providing support and advocacy for individuals with disabilities, and promoting inclusive policies and practices within the church and broader community.

Living Exhibit: The National Council of Churches' Disability Justice Initiatives

The National Council of Churches (NCC) has launched disability justice initiatives that integrate restorative justice principles. These initiatives include accessibility audits of church facilities, advocacy for inclusive policies, and support groups for individuals with disabilities and their families.

Intersectional Justice

Addressing Multiple Forms of Oppression

Intersectional justice recognizes that individuals often face multiple, overlapping forms of oppression. Christian communities are adopting an intersectional approach to restorative justice, addressing the complex and interconnected nature of social injustices.

Restorative Practices

Restorative practices that embrace intersectional justice include comprehensive support services, advocacy for intersectional policies, and educational programs that raise awareness about the interconnected nature of oppression.

Living Exhibit: The Intersectional Justice Program at Riverside Church

Riverside Church in New York City has developed an Intersectional Justice Program that integrates restorative justice with an intersectional approach to social justice. This program addresses issues such as racial inequality, gender discrimination, economic injustice, and environmental degradation through a holistic and interconnected framework.

Fostering Global Solidarity

International Restorative Justice Initiatives

Promoting Peace and Reconciliation Globally

Christian communities are engaging in restorative justice initiatives that promote peace and reconciliation on a global scale. These efforts involve supporting restorative practices in conflict-affected regions, advocating for international human rights, and building global partnerships for justice.

Living Exhibit: The Mennonite Central Committee's Global Peacebuilding Projects

The Mennonite Central Committee (MCC) has a long history of global peacebuilding projects that integrate restorative justice principles. These projects include conflict resolution training, support for displaced communities, and initiatives to rebuild trust and cooperation in post-conflict societies.

Supporting Restorative Justice Movements Worldwide

Sharing Resources and Expertise

Christian organizations are sharing resources, expertise, and best practices to support restorative justice movements worldwide. This global solidarity helps to strengthen restorative justice initiatives and promotes a collective commitment to justice and reconciliation.

Living Exhibit: The Global Restorative Justice Network

The Global Restorative Justice Network, supported by various Christian organizations, facilitates international collaboration on restorative justice. This network connects practitioners, researchers, and advocates, promoting the exchange of knowledge and best practices across borders.

Theological Reflection and Education

Deepening Theological Engagement with Social Justice

Integrating Theology and Practice

Christian communities are deepening their theological engagement with social justice issues, integrating restorative justice principles into their theological reflections and practices. This involves exploring biblical teachings on justice, mercy, and reconciliation in the context of contemporary social challenges.

Living Exhibit: Restorative Justice Seminars at Fuller Theological Seminary

Fuller Theological Seminary offers seminars and courses on restorative justice that integrate theological reflection with practical application. These programs engage students in exploring the theological foundations of restorative justice and its relevance to social justice movements.

Developing Theological Resources

Churches and Christian organizations are developing theological resources that support restorative justice practices and social justice advocacy. These resources include books, articles, study guides, and liturgical materials that help communities engage with restorative justice from a faith-based perspective.

Living Exhibit: Theological Publications by The Anabaptist Network

The Anabaptist Network publishes theological resources on restorative justice, drawing on the rich Anabaptist tradition of peacemaking and reconciliation. These publications provide theological insights and practical guidance for implementing restorative justice in Christian communities.

Educating and Training Leaders

Training Clergy and Lay Leaders

Educating and training clergy and lay leaders in restorative justice and social justice is essential for effective implementation. Churches are investing in leadership development programs that equip leaders with the knowledge and skills to facilitate restorative processes and advocate for social justice.

Living Exhibit: Restorative Justice Training by the United Church of Canada

The United Church of Canada offers restorative justice training for clergy and lay leaders, focusing on practical skills such as mediation, conflict resolution, and trauma-informed care. These training programs prepare leaders to implement restorative justice initiatives within their congregations and communities.

Promoting Lifelong Learning

Promoting lifelong learning about restorative justice and social justice is another important trend. Churches encourage ongoing education and professional development for those involved in these efforts, ensuring that they stay informed about best practices and emerging trends.

Living Exhibit: Continuing Education Programs at Wheaton College

Wheaton College offers continuing education programs in restorative justice and social justice, providing opportunities for practitioners to deepen their knowledge and skills. These programs include workshops, conferences, and online courses that support lifelong learning and professional growth.

Conclusion

The intersection of restorative justice with social justice movements reflects a dynamic and evolving field that integrates theological reflection, practical application, and engagement with broader societal challenges. Christian communities are increasingly addressing systemic injustices such as racial discrimination, economic inequality, and environmental degradation through restorative practices. By promoting inclusive and equitable practices, fostering global solidarity, and deepening theological engagement, churches are actively contributing to the development of restorative justice. These efforts demonstrate the ongoing commitment of Christian communities to promoting healing, reconciliation, and holistic justice in response to harm and conflict, reflecting the transformative power of the gospel in their practices.

CHAPTER 07

COMPARATIVE RELIGIOUS PERSPECTIVE

How Christian Views on Restorative Justice Compare with Other Religions

Introduction

Restorative justice is a concept that resonates across various religious traditions, each offering unique perspectives and practices. This chapter explores how Christian views on restorative justice compare with those of other major world religions, such as Judaism, Islam, Buddhism, and Hinduism. By examining these comparative perspectives, we can appreciate the commonalities and differences in how these faiths approach justice, reconciliation, and healing. Additionally, this chapter will argue why Christian restorative justice principles are particularly compelling within the broader religious landscape.

Comparative Perspectives on Restorative Justice

Judaism

Foundations in Torah and Talmud

Judaism's approach to justice is deeply rooted in the Torah and the Talmud. The Torah emphasizes justice (tzedek) and righteousness (tzedakah), while the Talmud elaborates on these principles through rabbinic interpretations.

Restitution and Repentance

Jewish law, or Halacha, emphasizes restitution and repentance. Offenders are required to make amends for their wrongdoings through compensation and sincere repentance. The concept of Teshuva (repentance) involves acknowledging the wrongdoing, seeking forgiveness, making restitution, and committing to change.

Restorative Practices

Restorative justice in Judaism includes practices such as community mediation and reconciliation rituals during Yom Kippur, the Day of Atonement. These practices underscore the importance of restoring relationships and community harmony.

Comparison with Christianity

While both Judaism and Christianity emphasize repentance and restitution, Christian restorative justice uniquely incorporates the sacrificial atonement of Jesus Christ as the foundation for forgiveness and reconciliation. This theological dimension provides a profound basis for transformative justice that goes beyond human efforts.

Islam

Foundations in the Quran and Hadith

Islamic views on justice are based on the Quran and the Hadith. The Quran emphasizes justice (adl) and mercy (rahmah), and the Hadith provide examples of how the Prophet Muhammad implemented these principles.

Restitution and Forgiveness

Islamic law, or Sharia, emphasizes both restitution and forgiveness. Offenders are expected to compensate for their wrongdoings and seek forgiveness from those they have harmed. The concept of Tawbah (repentance) involves sincere regret, seeking forgiveness from God and the victim, and making amends.

Restorative Practices

Restorative justice practices in Islam include Sulh (reconciliation) and Diyya (compensation). Sulh involves mediation to resolve conflicts and restore harmony, while

Diyya provides financial compensation to victims or their families for harm caused.

Comparison with Christianity

Islamic restorative justice shares similarities with Christian practices in emphasizing repentance and forgiveness. However, Christian restorative justice is deeply rooted in the life and teachings of Jesus, whose example of radical forgiveness and sacrificial love serves as a model for reconciliation. The concept of grace in Christianity offers a unique perspective that underscores the transformative power of divine forgiveness.

Buddhism

Foundations in the Dharma

Buddhism's approach to justice is based on the Dharma, the teachings of the Buddha. The Dharma emphasizes compassion (karuna), non-harming (ahimsa), and mindfulness.

Restitution and Mindfulness

Buddhist principles of justice involve acknowledging harm, making amends, and cultivating mindfulness and compassion. The practice of Right Action within the Noble Eightfold Path encourages ethical behavior and the resolution of conflicts through understanding and compassion.

Restorative Practices

Restorative justice in Buddhism includes practices such as mediation, mindfulness training, and community reconciliation ceremonies. These practices aim to heal relationships and promote inner peace and social harmony.

Comparison with Christianity

Buddhist restorative practices, like Christian ones, focus on healing and reconciliation. However, Christianity's emphasis on personal transformation through the grace of Jesus Christ adds a distinctive dimension. The narrative of Jesus' life, death, and resurrection provides a powerful framework for understanding and practicing restorative justice in a way that encompasses both divine and human elements.

Hinduism

Foundations in the Vedas and Upanishads

Hindu views on justice are informed by the Vedas, Upanishads, and other sacred texts. Hinduism emphasizes Dharma (righteousness) and Karma (the law of cause and effect).

Restitution and Karma

Hindu principles of justice involve making amends for wrongdoings and understanding the consequences of actions through the lens of Karma. The concept of Ahimsa (nonviolence) encourages resolving conflicts without harm and seeking reconciliation.

Restorative Practices

Restorative justice practices in Hinduism include rituals for atonement, mediation to resolve conflicts, and community ceremonies to restore harmony. These practices emphasize the interconnectedness of all beings and the importance of maintaining balance and order.

Comparison with Christianity

Hindu restorative justice practices share a focus on reconciliation and harmony with Christian practices. However, the Christian concept of grace and the emphasis on a personal relationship with God through Jesus Christ offer a unique perspective on restorative justice. This relationship provides believers with a profound sense of divine forgiveness and empowerment to seek reconciliation.

Why Christian Restorative Justice Principles are Compelling

The Centrality of Forgiveness

Forgiveness Rooted in Divine Grace

Christian restorative justice is compelling because it is deeply rooted in the concept of divine grace. The forgiveness offered through Jesus Christ is unconditional and transformative, providing a powerful foundation for reconciliation and healing. This divine forgiveness empowers individuals to extend forgiveness to others, creating a ripple effect of grace and restoration.

Living Exhibit: The Story of Corrie ten Boom

Corrie ten Boom, a Christian who survived a Nazi concentration camp, exemplified Christian forgiveness. After the war, she met one of her former guards and, through the power of Christ's forgiveness, was able to forgive him. Her story highlights the transformative power of Christian forgiveness in restorative justice.

The Emphasis on Reconciliation

Reconciliation as Central to the Gospel

Reconciliation is at the heart of the Christian gospel. The ministry of Jesus and the teachings of Paul emphasize restoring broken relationships between individuals, communities, and God. This emphasis on reconciliation provides a holistic approach to justice that seeks not only to address harm but also to restore wholeness.

Living Exhibit: The Reconciliation Ministry of Desmond Tutu

Archbishop Desmond Tutu's work in South Africa's Truth and Reconciliation Commission exemplifies the Christian commitment to reconciliation. His leadership in promoting forgiveness and healing after apartheid drew on

Christian principles, demonstrating the profound impact of reconciliation in restorative justice.

The Transformative Power of Love

Love as the Basis for Justice

Christian restorative justice is underpinned by the transformative power of love. Jesus' command to love one's neighbor as oneself and to love one's enemies forms the ethical foundation for restorative practices. This love is active, seeking to heal and restore rather than simply to punish.

Living Exhibit: The Civil Rights Movement

The American Civil Rights Movement, led by Christian leaders like Martin Luther King Jr., was deeply rooted in the principles of restorative justice and Christian love. King's philosophy of nonviolence and his emphasis on love and reconciliation had a profound impact on social justice, demonstrating the power of Christian restorative principles in addressing systemic injustices.

The Concept of Community

Building a Community of Believers

Christian restorative justice emphasizes the importance of community. The Church is seen as a body of believers who support one another, hold each other accountable, and work together towards reconciliation and healing. This communal approach ensures that restorative justice is not just an individual effort but a collective journey.

Living Exhibit: Restorative Practices in Mennonite Communities

Mennonite communities, with their strong emphasis on peace and reconciliation, provide a living exhibit of how Christian restorative justice can be practiced within a community. Their use of restorative circles, community dialogues, and mutual support highlights the importance of communal involvement in restorative justice.

Conclusion

Christian views on restorative justice, when compared with other religious traditions, offer unique and compelling principles that enhance the practice of justice, reconciliation, and healing. The centrality of forgiveness rooted in divine grace, the emphasis on reconciliation as integral to the gospel, the transformative power of love, and the concept of community all contribute to a holistic and profound approach to restorative justice. These principles, exemplified through powerful living exhibits, demonstrate the enduring impact of Christian restorative justice and its potential to transform individuals and societies. As Christian communities continue to engage with restorative justice, they offer a model that not only addresses harm but also fosters deep and lasting reconciliation and healing.

Interfaith Dialogue on Justice and Reconciliation

Introduction

Interfaith dialogue on justice and reconciliation involves the collaboration of different religious traditions to address issues of conflict, harm, and social injustice. These dialogues offer opportunities for mutual learning, shared values, and collaborative efforts in promoting restorative justice principles. This chapter explores how interfaith dialogues contribute to restorative justice, examines their effectiveness, and discusses what more can be done to enhance these efforts.

Interfaith Dialogue on Justice and Reconciliation

The Purpose and Goals of Interfaith Dialogue

Promoting Mutual Understanding

Interfaith dialogue aims to foster mutual understanding among different religious communities. By discussing their respective beliefs, practices, and perspectives on justice and reconciliation, participants can identify common ground and respect differences.

Building Relationships and Trust

Building relationships and trust is a key goal of interfaith dialogue. Through regular interactions and collaborative projects, religious communities can develop deeper connections and a sense of shared purpose in addressing social issues.

Collaborative Action for Social Justice

Interfaith dialogue often leads to collaborative action on social justice issues. By pooling resources and expertise, religious communities can address systemic injustices and promote restorative justice more effectively than working in isolation.

Examples of Interfaith Dialogue on Justice and Reconciliation

The Parliament of the World's Religions

The Parliament of the World's Religions is one of the largest interfaith gatherings globally, bringing together people of various faiths to discuss issues of peace, justice, and sustainability. It provides a platform for dialogue and collaboration on restorative justice initiatives.

Living Exhibit: The Toronto Parliament

At the 2018 Parliament of the World's Religions in Toronto, various workshops and panels focused on restorative justice. These sessions explored how different religious traditions approach justice and reconciliation and discussed ways to implement restorative practices in diverse communities.

The Interfaith Council of Metropolitan Washington (IFCMW)

The IFCMW brings together representatives from different faith traditions to promote dialogue and cooperation. Their initiatives include interfaith dialogues on social justice issues, collaborative community service projects, and educational programs.

Living Exhibit: The Interfaith Dialogue on Racial Justice

In response to rising racial tensions, the IFCMW organized an interfaith dialogue on racial justice. Participants from various religious backgrounds shared their perspectives on racism, discussed restorative justice approaches, and developed joint actions to promote racial reconciliation in their communities.

The United Religions Initiative (URI)

The URI is a global grassroots interfaith network that works to promote enduring daily interfaith cooperation, end religiously motivated violence, and create cultures of peace, justice, and healing. URI's initiatives include peacebuilding projects, educational programs, and advocacy for social justice.

Living Exhibit: URI's Peacebuilding in Nigeria

URI's work in Nigeria involves interfaith peacebuilding initiatives that address the conflict between Christian and Muslim communities. Through dialogue, mediation, and collaborative projects, URI promotes restorative justice and reconciliation, helping to heal divisions and build a more peaceful society.

The Impact of Interfaith Dialogue on Restorative Justice

Fostering a Shared Vision of Justice

Interfaith dialogues help to foster a shared vision of justice that transcends individual religious traditions. By focusing on common values such as compassion, forgiveness, and human dignity, these dialogues create a unified approach to restorative justice.

Enhancing Understanding and Empathy

Engaging with diverse religious perspectives enhances understanding and empathy among participants. This deeper understanding helps to address biases, reduce prejudices, and create a more inclusive approach to justice and reconciliation.

Strengthening Community Cohesion

Interfaith dialogue strengthens community cohesion by bringing together diverse groups to work towards common goals. This collaborative approach fosters a sense of solidarity and mutual support, which is essential for effective restorative justice practices.

Promoting Practical Collaboration

Interfaith dialogues often lead to practical collaboration on restorative justice initiatives. By combining resources and expertise, religious communities can implement more comprehensive and impactful restorative practices.

Living Exhibit: Interfaith Restorative Justice Programs in South Africa

In South Africa, interfaith dialogues have led to the development of restorative justice programs that address the legacy of apartheid. These programs involve Christian, Muslim, Jewish, and Indigenous communities working together to promote healing and reconciliation.

Challenges and Opportunities in Interfaith Dialogue

Challenges

Theological Differences

Theological differences can pose challenges to interfaith dialogue. Differing beliefs about justice, forgiveness, and reconciliation can create misunderstandings and hinder collaboration.

Power Imbalances

Power imbalances between different religious groups can affect the dynamics of interfaith dialogue. Dominant groups may inadvertently marginalize minority voices, affecting the inclusivity and effectiveness of the dialogue.

Historical Conflicts

Historical conflicts between religious communities can create distrust and reluctance to engage in dialogue. Addressing these historical grievances is essential for building trust and moving forward.

Opportunities

Leveraging Shared Values

Despite theological differences, many religious traditions share common values such as compassion, justice, and peace. Focusing on these shared values can create a strong foundation for collaborative efforts in restorative justice.

Inclusive Dialogue Practices

Adopting inclusive dialogue practices ensures that all voices are heard and respected. Facilitators should be trained to recognize and address power imbalances and create a safe space for open and honest communication.

Addressing Historical Grievances

Acknowledging and addressing historical grievances is crucial for building trust and fostering reconciliation. Interfaith dialogues should include discussions on past conflicts and explore ways to move towards healing and forgiveness.

Capacity Building

Investing in capacity building for religious leaders and communities can enhance the effectiveness of interfaith dialogues. Providing training on restorative justice principles, conflict resolution, and dialogue facilitation can empower participants to lead and sustain these efforts.

Enhancing the Impact of Interfaith Dialogue on Restorative Justice

Expanding Education and Awareness

Educational Programs

Expanding educational programs on restorative justice within religious communities can raise awareness and build support for these principles. Workshops, seminars, and study groups can help participants understand the importance of restorative justice and how it aligns with their faith.

Public Awareness Campaigns

Public awareness campaigns can promote the benefits of interfaith dialogue and restorative justice. Highlighting success stories and showcasing the positive impact of these initiatives can inspire broader community involvement.

Strengthening Partnerships

Collaborative Networks

Building collaborative networks that connect religious communities, NGOs, and governmental organizations can enhance the reach and impact of restorative justice initiatives. These networks can facilitate the sharing of resources, knowledge, and best practices.

Joint Advocacy Efforts

Joint advocacy efforts can amplify the voice of interfaith coalitions in promoting restorative justice policies. By working together, religious communities can influence legislative changes and promote systemic reforms that support restorative practices.

Promoting Long-Term Engagement

Sustained Dialogue

Promoting sustained dialogue rather than one-off events ensures ongoing engagement and relationship-building. Regular meetings, follow-up actions, and long-term projects can deepen trust and commitment to restorative justice.

Monitoring and Evaluation

Implementing monitoring and evaluation mechanisms can help assess the effectiveness of interfaith dialogues and restorative justice initiatives. Collecting data, gathering feedback, and making adjustments based on insights can improve the impact of these efforts.

Conclusion

Interfaith dialogue on justice and reconciliation plays a vital role in promoting restorative justice principles. By fostering mutual understanding, building relationships, and facilitating collaborative action, these dialogues contribute to a more inclusive and effective approach to addressing harm and conflict. Despite challenges such as theological differences and historical conflicts, the opportunities for shared learning and joint action are significant. To enhance the impact of interfaith dialogue on restorative justice, expanding education and awareness, strengthening partnerships, and promoting long-term engagement are essential steps. By continuing to engage in interfaith dialogue, religious communities can collectively work towards a more just, peaceful, and reconciled world.

CHAPTER 08

FUTURE DIRECTIONS

Emerging Trends and Future Possibilities in Christian Approaches to Restorative Justice

Introduction

As restorative justice continues to gain traction within Christian communities, emerging trends and future possibilities are shaping its evolution. This chapter explores these emerging trends and envisions future directions for Christian approaches to restorative justice. By examining innovative practices, expanding applications, and considering the potential impact of new developments, we can understand how Christian communities can further enhance their contributions to justice and reconciliation.

Emerging Trends in Christian Restorative Justice

Digital and Online Restorative Justice

Virtual Restorative Practices

The rise of digital communication technologies has opened new avenues for restorative justice practices. Virtual restorative circles, online mediation sessions, and digital storytelling platforms allow for restorative processes to occur across geographic boundaries, making them more accessible to diverse communities.

Living Exhibit: Online Restorative Justice Circles

During the COVID-19 pandemic, many churches and restorative justice organizations adapted by hosting online restorative justice circles. These virtual gatherings provided a space for individuals to share their experiences, seek reconciliation, and support one another despite physical distancing measures.

Expanding Reach

Digital platforms enable the inclusion of participants who might otherwise be unable to engage in traditional restorative processes due to distance, mobility issues, or other barriers. This expansion increases the reach and impact of restorative justice initiatives.

Integrating Restorative Justice into Institutional Frameworks

Restorative Practices in Schools

Christian schools are increasingly adopting restorative justice practices to address conflicts, bullying, and behavioral issues. These practices promote a positive school culture and teach students valuable skills in empathy, accountability, and conflict resolution.

Living Exhibit: Restorative Justice in Christian Schools

Many Christian schools have implemented restorative justice programs that include peer mediation, restorative circles, and conflict resolution training. These programs have led to reduced disciplinary issues, improved student relationships, and a more supportive school environment.

Restorative Approaches in Workplaces

Churches and Christian organizations are also exploring the integration of restorative justice principles into workplace settings. This involves addressing workplace conflicts, promoting ethical behavior, and fostering a culture of respect and collaboration.

Living Exhibit: Restorative Practices in Church Staff

Some churches have adopted restorative practices to address conflicts among staff members. By using mediation, facilitated dialogues, and team-building activities, these churches aim to create a harmonious and productive work environment.

Cross-Sector Collaboration

Partnerships with Secular Organizations

Increasingly, Christian communities are forming partnerships with secular organizations to advance restorative justice initiatives. These collaborations leverage the strengths and resources of both faith-based and secular entities to address complex social issues more effectively.

Living Exhibit: Interfaith and Secular Collaborations

Projects such as community mediation centers and restorative justice coalitions often involve collaboration between churches, non-profits, and government agencies. These partnerships enhance the scope and impact of restorative justice efforts by bringing together diverse perspectives and expertise.

Integrated Community Development

Restorative justice is being integrated into broader community development initiatives. This holistic approach addresses not only the immediate harm but also the underlying social and economic conditions that contribute to conflict and injustice.

Living Exhibit: Community Development Projects

Community development projects that incorporate restorative justice principles include initiatives focused on housing, education, and economic empowerment. These projects aim to create resilient communities where restorative practices are part of the fabric of everyday life.

Future Possibilities in Christian Restorative Justice

Expanding Theological Engagement

Deepening Theological Reflection

Future directions in Christian restorative justice involve deepening theological reflection on justice, forgiveness, and reconciliation. This includes exploring new interpretations of biblical texts, engaging with contemporary theological scholarship, and integrating insights from diverse theological traditions.

Living Exhibit: Theological Conferences on Restorative Justice

Theological conferences and symposiums dedicated to restorative justice provide platforms for scholars, clergy, and practitioners to share insights and develop new theological frameworks. These gatherings foster innovation and enrich the theological foundations of restorative justice.

Developing Contextual Theologies

Contextual theologies that address specific cultural, social, and historical contexts can enhance the relevance and effectiveness of restorative justice practices. These theologies draw on local traditions and experiences to inform and shape restorative approaches.

Living Exhibit: Indigenous Theologies of Restorative Justice

Indigenous Christian communities are developing theologies of restorative justice that integrate traditional practices with Christian teachings. These contextual theologies provide culturally resonant frameworks for reconciliation and healing.

Innovating Restorative Practices

Trauma-Informed Restorative Justice

Incorporating trauma-informed approaches into restorative justice practices is an emerging trend that acknowledges the complex impact of trauma on individuals and communities. Trauma-informed practices prioritize safety, empathy, and empowerment, creating a supportive environment for healing.

Living Exhibit: Trauma-Informed Restorative Circles

Restorative circles that incorporate trauma-informed principles include elements such as grounding exercises, clear communication guidelines, and access to mental health resources. These adaptations ensure that participants feel safe and supported throughout the restorative process.

Restorative Justice in Environmental Stewardship

Future possibilities for restorative justice include its application to environmental stewardship. Addressing environmental harm through restorative practices involves repairing ecosystems, advocating for sustainable practices, and fostering a sense of collective responsibility for creation care.

Living Exhibit: Environmental Restoration Projects

Church-led environmental restoration projects, such as reforestation efforts, river clean-ups, and sustainable agriculture initiatives, integrate restorative justice principles. These projects emphasize repairing harm to the environment and promoting ecological balance.

Enhancing Global Engagement

Global Restorative Justice Networks

Building and strengthening global restorative justice networks can enhance the exchange of knowledge, resources, and best practices across different contexts. These networks facilitate international collaboration and support the growth of restorative justice movements worldwide.

Living Exhibit: Global Restorative Justice Conferences

Global conferences on restorative justice bring together practitioners, researchers, and advocates from around the world. These events provide opportunities for learning, networking, and collaborative action on a global scale.

Supporting Restorative Justice in Conflict Zones

Christian communities can play a significant role in supporting restorative justice initiatives in conflict zones. This involves providing resources, training, and advocacy to promote peacebuilding and reconciliation in areas affected by violence and instability.

Living Exhibit: Peacebuilding in Post-Conflict Societies

Christian organizations engaged in peacebuilding efforts in post-conflict societies use restorative justice principles to facilitate dialogue, rebuild trust, and promote healing. These initiatives contribute to long-term peace and stability.

Leveraging Technology and Innovation

Utilizing Artificial Intelligence

The use of artificial intelligence (AI) in restorative justice is an emerging possibility. AI can help analyze conflict patterns, provide data-driven insights, and support the design of tailored restorative interventions. However, ethical considerations must guide the use of AI to ensure it aligns with restorative justice principles.

Living Exhibit: AI-Supported Mediation Platforms

AI-supported mediation platforms use machine learning algorithms to facilitate conflict resolution processes.

These platforms can analyze communication patterns, suggest mediation strategies, and support facilitators in managing complex dialogues.

Virtual Reality for Empathy Building

Virtual reality (VR) technology offers innovative ways to build empathy and understanding in restorative justice practices. VR experiences can immerse participants in the perspectives of others, fostering deeper emotional connections and enhancing the restorative process.

Living Exhibit: VR Empathy Workshops

VR empathy workshops use virtual reality to simulate experiences of harm and reconciliation. Participants can engage in immersive scenarios that help them understand the impact of their actions and the importance of restorative justice.

Conclusion

The future of Christian approaches to restorative justice is marked by innovation, expansion, and deepening engagement. Emerging trends such as digital restorative practices, cross-sector collaboration, and trauma-informed approaches are transforming how restorative justice is implemented within Christian communities. Future possibilities include expanding theological engagement, innovating restorative practices, enhancing global networks, and leveraging technology. By embracing these trends and possibilities, Christian communities can continue to advance restorative justice, promoting healing, reconciliation, and holistic justice in response to harm and conflict. As they do so, they reflect the transformative power of the gospel and contribute to the building of a more just, peaceful, and compassionate world.

Recommendations for Individuals and Communities

Introduction

Restorative justice offers a transformative approach to addressing harm, promoting healing, and restoring relationships. As Christian communities seek to deepen their engagement with restorative justice principles, it is essential to consider practical recommendations for individuals and communities. This chapter provides actionable steps and strategies that can help integrate restorative justice into daily life and community practices.

Recommendations for Individuals

Personal Reflection and Growth

1. Educate Yourself

Gain a thorough understanding of restorative justice principles and practices. Read books, attend workshops, and participate in discussions to deepen your knowledge and awareness.

2. Reflect on Personal Experiences

Consider how restorative justice principles can apply to your personal experiences of conflict and harm. Reflect on past situations where forgiveness, accountability, and reconciliation could have made a difference.

3. Practice Active Listening

Develop your skills in active listening, a core component of restorative justice. This involves listening without judgment, being fully present, and showing empathy towards others.

4. Seek Forgiveness and Reconciliation

Take steps to seek forgiveness and reconciliation in your relationships. Acknowledge any harm you may have caused, apologize sincerely, and strive to make amends.

Building Restorative Habits

5. Foster a Forgiving Attitude

Cultivate a forgiving attitude in your daily interactions. Let go of grudges and practice compassion towards those who have wronged you.

6. Promote Open Communication

Encourage open and honest communication in your relationships. Create a safe space where others feel comfortable expressing their thoughts and feelings.

7. Model Restorative Practices

Lead by example by modeling restorative practices in your interactions. Show how to handle conflicts constructively and promote healing and reconciliation.

Engaging in Community Activities

8. Participate in Restorative Justice Initiatives

Get involved in restorative justice initiatives in your community. Volunteer with organizations that promote restorative practices or join local mediation and reconciliation efforts.

9. Advocate for Restorative Justice

Advocate for restorative justice in your community and beyond. Speak out about the benefits of restorative approaches and encourage others to adopt these practices.

10. Support Victims and Offenders

Provide support to both victims and offenders in restorative justice processes. Offer empathy, encouragement, and practical assistance to help them navigate the journey towards healing and reconciliation.

Recommendations for Communities

Fostering a Restorative Culture

1. Educate and Train Members

Provide education and training on restorative justice for all community members. Offer workshops, seminars, and resources that explain restorative principles and how to apply them.

2. Establish Restorative Policies

Develop and implement policies that promote restorative justice within the community. This includes creating guidelines for handling conflicts, addressing harm, and facilitating reconciliation processes.

3. Create Safe Spaces for Dialogue

Designate safe spaces where community members can engage in open dialogue about conflicts and harm. Ensure that these spaces are welcoming and accessible to all.

Implementing Restorative Practices

4. Form Restorative Justice Teams

Form teams of trained individuals who can facilitate restorative justice processes. These teams can include mediators, counselors, and community leaders who are skilled in restorative practices.

5. Conduct Restorative Circles and Mediation

Regularly conduct restorative circles and mediation sessions to address conflicts and harm. Encourage participation from all affected parties and focus on healing and reconciliation.

6. Integrate Restorative Justice in Schools

Implement restorative justice programs in local schools. Educate students, teachers, and staff on restorative principles and provide practical tools for resolving conflicts and promoting a positive school culture.

Building Partnerships and Collaborations

7. Collaborate with Local Organizations

Build partnerships with local organizations that support restorative justice. Collaborate on projects, share resources, and create a network of support for restorative initiatives.

8. Engage with Legal and Governmental Systems

Work with legal and governmental systems to promote restorative justice. Advocate for policies that support restorative approaches and collaborate on community-based justice initiatives.

9. Involve Faith Leaders

Involve faith leaders in restorative justice efforts. Their influence and guidance can help integrate restorative principles into the spiritual life of the community.

Monitoring and Evaluation

10. Regularly Assess Restorative Efforts

Regularly assess the effectiveness of restorative justice efforts in the community. Gather feedback from participants, track outcomes, and make adjustments as needed to improve processes.

11. Celebrate Successes

Celebrate the successes of restorative justice initiatives. Share stories of healing and reconciliation to inspire others and highlight the positive impact of restorative practices.

12. Provide Ongoing Support

Provide ongoing support for restorative justice efforts. Ensure that facilitators, participants, and community members have access to the resources and assistance they need to continue promoting healing and reconciliation.

Conclusion

Integrating restorative justice into individual and community practices requires commitment, education, and collaboration. By following these recommendations, individuals can develop restorative habits and contribute to a culture of healing and reconciliation. Communities can foster restorative environments by educating members, implementing practices, building partnerships, and continually assessing their efforts. Through these collective actions, Christian communities can embody the principles of restorative justice, reflecting the transformative power of the gospel and contributing to a more just and compassionate world.

APPENDIX A

RESOURCES FOR FURTHER READINGS

Appendix: Resources for Further Reading

Books on Restorative Justice

1. "The Little Book of Restorative Justice" by Howard Zehr

- A foundational text that introduces the principles and practices of restorative justice. Zehr is considered one of the pioneers in the field, and this book is essential for understanding the basics.

2. "Changing Lenses: Restorative Justice for Our Times" by Howard Zehr

- This book offers a deeper exploration of restorative justice, comparing it to traditional criminal justice approaches and advocating for systemic change.

3. "The Little Book of Biblical Justice: A Fresh Approach to the Bible's Teachings on Justice" by Chris Marshall

- This book integrates biblical teachings with restorative justice principles, providing a Christian perspective on justice and reconciliation.

4. "The Little Book of Restorative Discipline for Schools: Teaching Responsibility; Creating Caring Climates" by Lorraine Stutzman Amstutz and Judy H. Mullet

- A practical guide for implementing restorative justice in educational settings, focusing on creating positive school environments.

5. "Restoring Justice: An Introduction to Restorative Justice" by Daniel W. Van Ness and Karen Heetderks Strong

- A comprehensive introduction to restorative justice, including its history, theoretical foundations, and practical applications.

6. "The Church of the Future: Restorative Justice and the Reconciliation of All Things" by Michael J. Holt

- Explores the role of the church in promoting restorative justice and how it aligns with the broader mission of reconciliation.

7. "Restorative Justice: Ideals and Realities" by Margarita Zernova

- This book critically examines the implementation of restorative justice, discussing both its potential and the challenges it faces.

Articles and Journals

1. "Restorative Justice: The Evidence" by Lawrence W. Sherman and Heather Strang

- An evidence-based review of restorative justice practices and their effectiveness, available as a publication from the University of Cambridge.

2. "Restorative Justice and the Biblical Tradition" by Daniel Van Ness

- This article explores how restorative justice principles align with biblical teachings, offering theological insights for Christian communities.

3. "The Justice That Heals: A Biblical Vision of Restorative Justice" by Chris Marshall

- Published in various theological journals, this article delves into the biblical foundations of restorative justice.

Online Resources

1. Restorative Justice International (RJI)

- Website: [restorativejusticeinternational.com](https://www.restorativejusticeinternational.com)

- A global community of restorative justice practitioners and advocates, offering resources, news, and networking opportunities.

2. The Center for Justice and Reconciliation

-   Website: [restorativejustice.org](https://www.restorativejustice.org)

- Provides educational materials, case studies, and research on restorative justice.

3. Restorative Justice Online

- Website: [rjonline.org](https://www.rjonline.org)

- An online hub for resources, articles, and discussion forums on restorative justice.

4. The International Institute for Restorative Practices (IIRP)

- Website: [iirp.edu](https://www.iirp.edu)

- Offers training, research, and publications on restorative practices, including an online library of resources.

Educational Programs and Courses

1. Fuller Theological Seminary - Restorative Justice Courses

- Website: [fuller.edu](https://www.fuller.edu)

- Offers courses and seminars that integrate theological education with restorative justice principles.

2. Eastern Mennonite University - Center for Justice and Peacebuilding

- Website: [emu.edu/cjp](https://www.emu.edu/cjp)

- Provides graduate programs and training in restorative justice and conflict transformation.

3. The University of Vermont - Certificate in Restorative Practices

- Website: [learn.uvm.edu](https://learn.uvm.edu/program/restorative-practices-certificate)

- Offers an online certificate program in restorative practices, covering theory and practical application.

4. The University of Hull - MA in Restorative Justice

- Website: [hull.ac.uk](https://www.hull.ac.uk/study/postgraduate/taught/restorative-justice-ma)

- Provides a master's degree program focused on the study and application of restorative justice.

Conferences and Workshops

1. The Restorative Justice Conference

- An annual event bringing together practitioners, researchers, and advocates to discuss the latest developments in restorative justice. Check online for dates and locations.

2. The International Conference on Restorative Practices

- Organized by the International Institute for Restorative Practices, this conference covers a wide range of topics related to restorative justice and practices.

3. National Association of Community and Restorative Justice (NACRJ) Conference

- Website: [nacrj.org](https://www.nacrj.org)

- Biennial conference focusing on community and restorative justice, offering workshops, presentations, and networking opportunities.

Organizations and Advocacy Groups

1. Prison Fellowship International

- Website: [pfi.org](https://www.pfi.org)

- A Christian organization that promotes restorative justice through various programs and initiatives worldwide.

2. Mennonite Central Committee (MCC)

- Website: [mcc.org](https://www.mcc.org)

- Engages in peacebuilding and restorative justice projects globally, providing resources and support for communities.

3. The Catholic Mobilizing Network

-   Website:
[catholicsmobilizing.org](https://www.catholicsmobilizing.org)

   - Advocates for restorative justice and the abolition of the death penalty, offering educational resources and advocacy tools.

Conclusion

This appendix provides a comprehensive list of resources for further reading on restorative justice, offering a range of books, articles, online resources, educational programs, conferences, and organizations. These resources will help individuals and communities deepen their understanding of restorative justice and explore practical ways to integrate these principles into their lives and practices.

APPENDIX B

PRACTICAL GUIDES FOR IMPLEMENTING RESTORATIVE JUSTICE PRINCIPLES

Implementing restorative justice principles requires practical tools and strategies that can be adapted to various contexts. This appendix provides step-by-step guides, tips, and resources for individuals, communities, schools, and organizations to effectively integrate restorative justice into their practices.

Step-by-Step Guide for Individuals

1. Educate Yourself on Restorative Justice

- Read Foundational Texts: Start with introductory books such as "The Little Book of Restorative Justice" by Howard Zehr.

- Attend Workshops and Seminars: Participate in local or online restorative justice workshops to gain practical skills.

- Join Discussion Groups: Engage with others interested in restorative justice through forums, book clubs, or study groups.

2. Reflect on Personal Experiences

- Identify Past Conflicts: Think about conflicts or harms you have experienced or caused.

- Consider Restorative Approaches: Reflect on how restorative practices like dialogue and reconciliation could have been applied.

3. Practice Active Listening and Empathy

- Listen Without Interrupting: Focus on understanding the speaker's perspective without judgment.

- Show Empathy: Express understanding and compassion towards others' feelings and experiences.

4. Seek Forgiveness and Reconciliation

- Acknowledge Harm: If you have harmed someone, acknowledge your actions and their impact.

- Apologize Sincerely: Offer a genuine apology and express your desire to make amends.

- Make Restitution: Take concrete steps to repair the harm, if possible.

Practical Tips for Communities

1. Educate and Train Community Members

- Host Workshops: Organize restorative justice workshops for community members.

- Provide Resources: Distribute books, articles, and online materials on restorative justice.

- Invite Experts: Bring in restorative justice practitioners to share their experiences and insights.

2. Establish Restorative Policies and Practices

- Develop Guidelines: Create guidelines for addressing conflicts and harm within the community.

- Form Restorative Teams: Assemble teams of trained facilitators who can lead restorative processes.

- Integrate into Community Events: Incorporate restorative practices into regular community events and meetings.

3. Create Safe Spaces for Dialogue

- Designate Meeting Areas: Identify spaces where restorative dialogues and circles can take place.

- Ensure Inclusivity: Make sure these spaces are welcoming and accessible to all community members.

- Promote Confidentiality: Establish and maintain confidentiality to create a safe environment for open dialogue.

4. Monitor and Evaluate Efforts

- Collect Feedback: Regularly gather feedback from participants in restorative processes.

- Assess Outcomes: Evaluate the effectiveness of restorative practices in resolving conflicts and promoting healing.

- Make Adjustments: Use feedback and assessment results to improve restorative justice initiatives.

Implementing Restorative Justice in Schools

1. Introduce Restorative Justice to Staff and Students

- Professional Development: Provide training for teachers and staff on restorative justice principles.

- Student Workshops: Organize workshops for students to learn about restorative practices.

- Incorporate into Curriculum: Integrate restorative justice concepts into relevant subjects such as social studies and ethics.

2. Establish Restorative Practices

- Restorative Circles: Use restorative circles to address conflicts, build community, and foster dialogue.

- Peer Mediation: Train students as peer mediators to help resolve conflicts among their peers.

- Restorative Conferences: Hold restorative conferences for more serious incidents, involving all affected parties in a facilitated dialogue.

3. Create a Supportive Environment

- Promote a Positive School Culture: Encourage a school culture that values respect, empathy, and accountability.

- Provide Support Services: Offer counseling and support services for students involved in restorative processes.

- Engage Parents and Guardians: Involve parents and guardians in restorative justice initiatives and keep them informed about the school's approach.

Integrating Restorative Justice in Organizations

1. Educate and Train Employees

- Workshops and Training Sessions: Provide restorative justice training for employees at all levels.

- Develop Resource Libraries: Create a library of restorative justice resources for employees to access.

- Invite Speakers: Host talks and seminars with restorative justice experts.

2. Implement Restorative Policies and Procedures

- Conflict Resolution Policies: Develop policies that prioritize restorative approaches to resolving workplace conflicts.

- Restorative Committees: Form committees dedicated to implementing and overseeing restorative justice practices.

- Mediation Services: Offer mediation services to address disputes between employees.

3. Foster a Restorative Workplace Culture

- Encourage Open Communication: Promote a culture of open and honest communication.

- Model Restorative Leadership: Encourage leaders to model restorative practices in their interactions.

- Recognize and Reward: Recognize and reward employees who actively contribute to a restorative workplace culture.

4. Evaluate and Improve Practices

- Gather Feedback: Collect feedback from employees about their experiences with restorative justice processes.

- Monitor Outcomes: Track the outcomes of restorative practices and their impact on workplace dynamics.

- Continuous Improvement: Use feedback and data to continuously improve restorative justice initiatives.

Resources and Tools for Implementation

1. Books and Articles

- "The Little Book of Restorative Justice" by Howard Zehr

- "Restoring Justice: An Introduction to Restorative Justice" by Daniel W. Van Ness and Karen Heetderks Strong

- "The Little Book of Restorative Discipline for Schools" by Lorraine Stutzman Amstutz and Judy H. Mullet

2. Online Platforms and Networks

- Restorative Justice International (RJI)

- Website: [restorativejusticeinternational.com](https://www.restorativejusticeinternational.com)

- The Center for Justice and Reconciliation

- Website: [restorativejustice.org](https://www.restorativejustice.org)

- The International Institute for Restorative Practices (IIRP)

- Website: [iirp.edu](https://www.iirp.edu)

3. Training Programs and Workshops

- Fuller Theological Seminary - Restorative Justice Courses

- Website: [fuller.edu](https://www.fuller.edu)

- Eastern Mennonite University - Center for Justice and Peacebuilding

- Website: [emu.edu/cjp](https://www.emu.edu/cjp)

- The University of Vermont - Certificate in Restorative Practices

Website:
[learn.uvm.edu](https://learn.uvm.edu/program/restorative
-practices-certificate)

4. Support and Counseling Services

- Local Counseling Centers

- Faith-Based Support Groups

- Professional Mediation Services

Conclusion

Implementing restorative justice principles requires commitment, education, and practical strategies. By following the step-by-step guides and utilizing the resources provided, individuals and communities can effectively integrate restorative justice into their practices. These efforts will promote healing, reconciliation, and a culture of justice and compassion, reflecting the transformative power of restorative justice principles in action.

www.ingramcontent.com/pod-product-compliance
Lightning Source LLC
Chambersburg PA
CBHW061248120726
48001CB00001B/200